CARAVANS OF THE HIMALAYA

PUBLISHED BY

THE NATIONAL GEOGRAPHIC SOCIETY

Gilbert M. Grosvenor
President and Chairman of the Board

Michela A. English
Senior Vice President

BOOK DIVISION

William R. Gray
Vice President and Director

Charles Kogod
Assistant Director

EDITORIAL STAFF

Ron Fisher, *Editor*
**Danielle M. Beauchamp, M. Barbara Brownell,
Diane Coleman, Mary B. Dickinson,
Timothy H. Ewing, Sandra F. Lotterman,
Carl Mehler, Peter Miller, Suzanne Moyer,
Joseph F. Ochlak, Barbara Payne,
Lyle Rosbotham, Cinda Rose**

This book was made possible by the assistance of Lakpa Gyalzen Sherpa.

*Front endpapers:
A traditional
depiction of Dolpo
and the summertime
activities of its
people.*

*Pages 2-3: The
valley of the
Panzang River,
which runs parallel
to the Chinese
border.*

© 1994 Éditions de La Martinière (Paris, France)
ISBN: 2-73-242 079-4
Dépot légal : 2ème semestre 1994

Printed in France

CARAVANS
OF THE
HIMALAYA

CARAVANS
OF THE
HIMALAYA

Eric Valli and Diane Summers

Illustrations : Lama Tenzing Norbu

National Geographic Society
Washington, D. C.

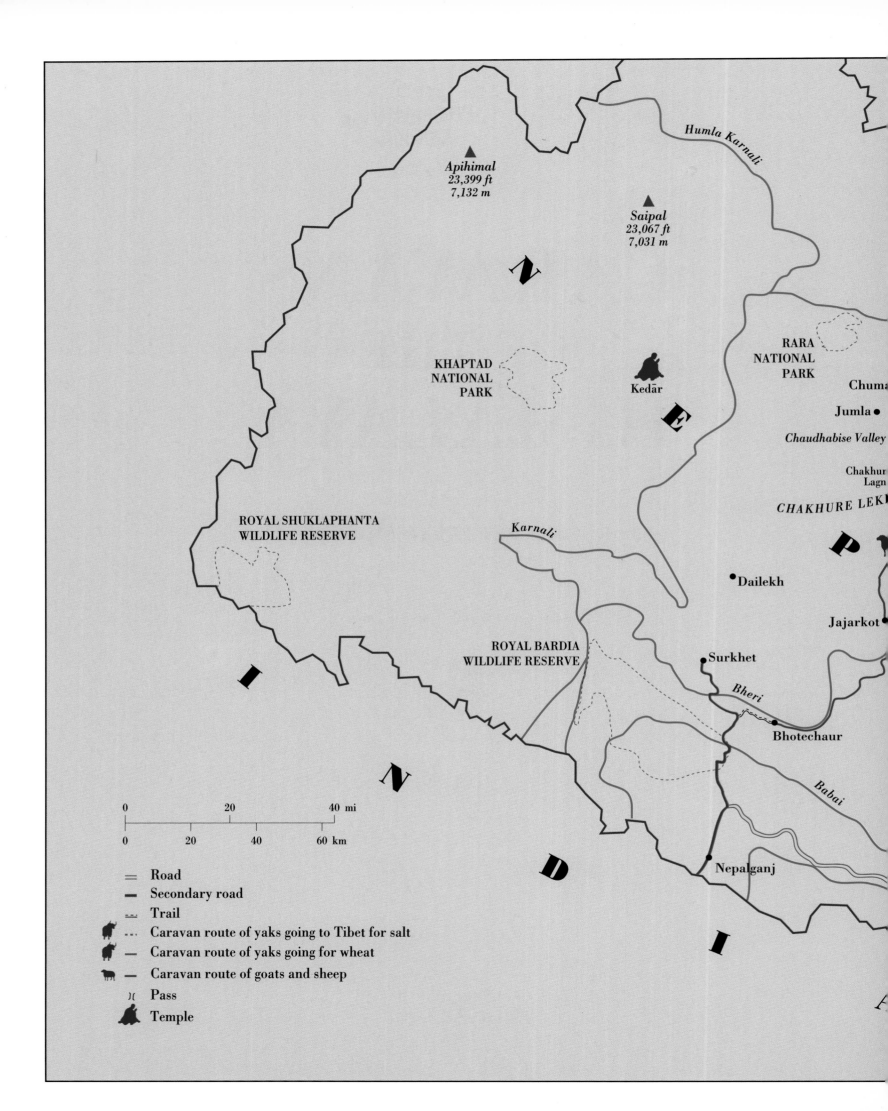

Apihimal
23,399 ft
7,132 m

Saipal
23,067 ft
7,031 m

Humla Karnali

N

RARA
NATIONAL
PARK

Chuma

KHAPTAD
NATIONAL
PARK

Kedār

E

Jumla •

Chaudhabise Valley

Chakhur
Lagn

ROYAL SHUKLAPHANTA
WILDLIFE RESERVE

Karnali

CHAKHURE LEK

P

• Dailekh

I

ROYAL BARDIA
WILDLIFE RESERVE

Surkhet

Jajarkot

Bheri

Bhotechaur

N

Babai

D

Nepalganj

I

=	Road
▬	Secondary road
--	Trail
⋯	Caravan route of yaks going to Tibet for salt
—	Caravan route of yaks going for wheat
—	Caravan route of goats and sheep
)(	Pass
🛕	Temple

Scale:
0 — 20 — 40 mi
0 — 20 — 40 — 60 km

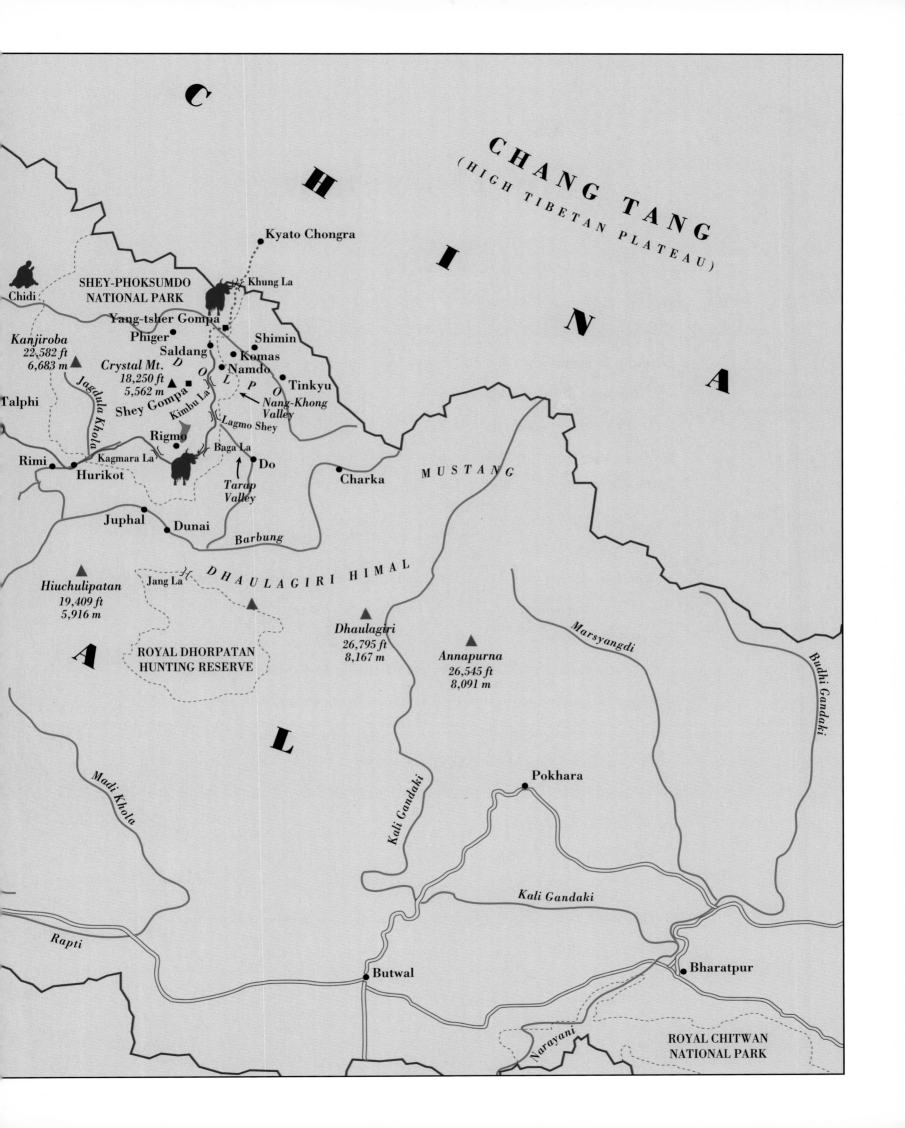

The Horseman

It happened in 1981 during my first visit to Dolpo. I was walking alone near the Dechen Labrang monastery, when a horseman galloped toward me. He wore a dark blue silk *chuba* and sported a fox-fur cap. His stirrups were sculpted, his saddlecloth rich, and his felt boots were embroidered. He stopped in front of me and, without dismounting, exclaimed haughtily:

chuba:
a Tibetan overcoat

"What are you doing here?"

"I came to see your country."

"Do you have a pass?"

I did not. At that time, Dolpo was forbidden to foreigners, and I did not have the authorization to be there. I took my only chance:

"Do you think that I would be here if I had not?"

He looked straight into my eyes, puzzled and silent. Then he smiled, whipped his pony, and disappeared as quickly as he had come.

I often think about that horseman.

I am grateful that he scorned all the barriers man builds so often between himself and his fellowmen. I am grateful that, in his own way, he accepted me among his fellowmen.

Thus began a great adventure.

This book is dedicated to all tolerant people, and especially to the Himalayan people.

ཞལ་ཁ།

Journey to the Hidden Land

The sky will be my roof; the earth my bed;

The grass, my soft pillow.

Like the clouds and the streams

I will traverse these immense deserts alone.

—Ekai Kawaguchi

Ekai Kawaguchi: Japanese Buddhist, the first foreigner to visit Dolpo, in 1890.

4.30 p.m. Diane and I just crossed the pass of Jang La. The landscape is splendid. It is a lunar landscape, a desert. In the blue Himalayan sky, flakelike clouds play with light along the purple and ocher escarpments that stretch toward Tibet's snowed-in summits. I listen to the silence, a deafening humming coming from deep inside this mineral universe.

DOLPO

When had I first heard about this isolated, mysterious region, which is forbidden to foreigners? I do not remember. For the past ten years at least, whenever I can, I return to Dolpo.

Eric behind the salt sacks with our caravan companions.

I arrive safe and sound, and like all the pilgrims and travelers who

11

penetrate Dolpo, I deposit a white stone and some dried fruit on the cairn as an offering to the local gods.

"*Sooo! Sooo! Lha gyalo!*—May the gods be victorious!" The prayer flags flap in the wind. The coldness chills me to the bone. I run down the slope shouting, drunk with joy and freedom.

But I am also afraid. I write to my parents: "I will be back in December if the winter does not take me into its white arms."

Dolpo is a world apart. The ancient Central Asian lifestyle survives in the high, solitary valleys of western Nepal.

To the south lie the gigantic walls of ice and rocks with the world's highest summits and highest passes: the Himalaya. To the north is the high Tibetan Plateau called Chang Tang, the desert of grass swept by storms and furrowed by the changing waters of the *Tsangpo*. The Tsangpo empties just like the Ganges into the Gulf of Bengal after making

Diane and Tsultria en route to Shey.

Tsangpo: Tibetan name of the Brahmaputra River

an unbelievable detour around the mountains. According to legend, Dolpo is a Be-yul, a hidden land, that was discovered by *Guru Rimpoche*, the great master who brought Buddhism from India to Tibet in the eighth century. During his epic voyage through the Himalaya, he subjugated the gods and demons reigning over the lands. He discovered sacred places that were difficult to reach and that were protected from the outside world by high mountains or profound forests. They have been spiritual places of refuge for the generations that followed.

Guru Rimpoche:
Padmasambhava

Even today, the journey to Dolpo is not easy. Once one leaves the road, one has to hike for three weeks on narrow and winding trails to reach the heart of the country. One must cross several passes more than 16,000 feet high in weather conditions that can change from one hour to the next, from burning sun to an unpredictable storm. Many *Dolpo-pa* have lost their lives in such storms. Like the Dolpo-pa, I thanked the gods for their clemency after crossing each pass. The Dolpo spent centuries ignored by foreigners. A Japanese monk was the first foreigner to enter Dolpo, in 1890. Dressed as a lama, he passed through this region without authorization and reached Tibet to study Buddhist texts. He had only the bare minimum with him. According to the monk, he only had "the snow as a place to sleep and a rock as a pillow." Kawaguchi was surprised that men could survive in a place as inhospitable and isolated as Dolpo, but he still remained sensitive to the savage beauty of the place: "I must not forget to pay homage to this grandiose nature: the summits with eternal snow, the gigantic mass of jagged rocks, the quietude of the place, all of it imposing fear and elevating the soul." *

Dolpo-pa:
a person of Dolpo

* *Ekai Kawaguchi,*
Three Years in Tibet

Only a handful of visitors followed Kawaguchi. During the 1920s, two cartographers sketched the region for the *Survey of India*. After World War II, the geologist Tony Hagen traversed Dolpo, and a botanist studied

Survey of India:
first cartography of
the Himalaya

the flora. In spite of the curiosity of some adventurers, mountaineers, scientists, and explorers, this Nepalese region has largely been ignored. The Western world finally became conscious of its existence following the sojourn of the Tibetologist David Snellgrove in 1956. For the first time, Dolpo was displayed on a map.

While Kawaguchi only crossed Dolpo, Snellgrove stayed more than a year in the Hidden Land. Fifty years had passed since the visit of the Japanese monk, but nothing had changed. The desert and isolated villages were still there. "We admired this splendid landscape, which was different from all that I had visited in the Himalaya." *

David Snellgrove, Himalayan Pilgrimage

During the 1960s, French ethnologist Corneille Jest shared the "harsh daily life of these men who seemed to have risen from the dawn of time." *

Corneille Jest, Tarap, a Valley in the Himalaya

In spite of its ties with the Hindu kingdom of Jumla in the west, Dolpo, which is located on the northern slope of the Himalaya, used to be an integral part of Tibet and had very close ties with the kingdom of Lho (Mustang) to the east, a western province of the Snowland.

At the end of the 18th century, Pritivin Narayan Shah, the sovereign of the minuscule southern kingdom of Gurkha, gradually conquered the numerous neighboring principalities to form today's Nepal. He conquered the Kathmandu Valley and turned his forces to the west. Jumla and Lho could not win against Gurkha's strong forces and succumbed. Dolpo was absorbed under the Kathmandu rule without troops even reaching it.

The Hidden Land was then governed by new masters of a new religion—Hinduism—from a faraway capital. The new rulers were not interested in this isolated region, except when it came to taxing salt. The daily life of Dolpo continued without much change.

The Dolpo-pa continued to go to Tibet for grazing and exchanging

grain for the salt of the Drok-pa, nomadic people from the highlands.

In the 1950s, the invasion of Tibet by China and the opening of Nepal to the modern world and tourism radically transformed the culture and economy of the Himalayan lands. Dolpo, however, was spared this. Its geographical position kept it isolated from these great changes. Dolpo did not betray its Be-yul legend. During the 1970s, the American writer Peter Matthiessen accompanied zoologist George Schaller in his study of the blue *bharal* of Tibet. Peter Matthiessen wrote: "Dolpo, all but unknown to Westerners even today, was said to be the last enclave of pure Tibetan culture....Its people [enjoy] a way of life that cannot differ much from that of the Ch'ang Tartars out of Central Asia who are thought to have been the original Tibetans, and their speech echoes the tongue of nomads who may have arrived two thousand years ago." *

bharal:
wild Tibetan sheep

* **Peter Matthiessen,**
The Snow Leopard

I wanted to know this land. I wanted to share the life of these people and melt into this savage nature. I wanted to go where the heart of Tibet still beats, and where life passes to the rhythm of yak caravans.

The village of Saldang, under the mantle of winter's snow.

Sara

After verifying several times that he is not mistaken, Labrang Tundup lifts his eyes from his divination book. We await his verdict.

"Her breath of life is strong enough," the diviner says slowly, "but the sickness is not finished...."

Tundup is 45 years old. He is refined and elegant. His leathery skin, almond-shaped eyes, and high cheekbones speak of Tibetan ancestry. Disorderly strands of hair escape the plait wound around his forehead. He is the *amchi*, the doctor and shaman of Saldang.

*amchi:
Tibetan doctor*

All this is a bit crazy, being in the hands of a Himalayan shaman!

Of course we tried our customary cures, aspirin and antacid, but nothing worked. We no longer know how to cure our four-year-old daughter, Sara. She has not eaten for several days and complains of abdominal pain. Is it gastroenteritis, appendicitis, or indigestion?

Sara plays with a yak horn while in a basket on the back of a pack animal.

During the night her fever gets higher, and her little hands draw circles in the semidarkness of the chapel where we sleep and where the bronze gods look at the three of us lying on the floor.

■ SARA ■

*Labrang Tundup,
the Tibetan doctor,
in a sheepskin
overcoat.*

"Mummy, Mummy," she murmurs softly.

We take her into our arms to comfort and reassure her. But she does not hear us. During the day, she lies in the shade in a corner of the flat roof of Tundup's house. The pony she so badly wanted to ride no longer interests her. Her eyes have dark circles under them. She has lost all her vitality. Diane and I are very worried.

This morning, after a sleepless night, I go to the roof. The first rays of the sun already illuminate the bottom of the valley. I see two small green patches: two villages and a barley field, two tiny oases almost invisible in the midst of this mountain desert. What are we doing here? How long would it take to escape this place? Days and days. How many children die young in this country?

I do not know one family that has not lost at least one child. Several months ago I visited some good friends. I was surprised when I did not see their three-year-old son.

"He fell sick," said his mother. "His body dried up until only the bones were left. Then he died. But we have a newborn," she added with joy, showing me the tiny baby wrapped in a blanket. Tundup had offered to help us. I have known him for many years. I have often stayed and traveled with him. One winter he even came to see us in Kathmandu. He is an honest person, respected for his competence. In Dolpo, everybody knows his reputation, and we are privileged to be among his friends.

While Camille, our second daughter, plays with the village children, Tundup suggests a *mo*, a divination. Why would this little *go serpo* be the victim of an illness?

go serpo:
"yellow head,"
thus, any Westerner

The shaman unwraps three small ivory dice from a piece of fabric and closes his right hand over them. His head thrown back and his

(pages 24-25) *Karma and other villagers aim for the demon's heart, to kill the evil spirits that are hurting Sara.*

Tilen Lhundrup worries about Sara's fever in his tent.

eyes closed, he invokes the protective deities. His wrist draws slow circles. He touches his forehead three times, drops the dice into a porcelain cup, and examines the result. His divination book is open to the page corresponding to the number on the dice. He then declares: "Sara belongs to an important clan. She wears nice clothes and eats well. She has crossed the passes on the back of a pack animal and has attracted the attention of a *lhu*, an underground divinity. This is why she is sick. We must do a *kurim*, an exorcism."

This is not a good day for an exorcism. All the monks have left for Yang-tsher for the mid-summer festival. Only Parme Tuwa has stayed behind to chase the hail that can menace the harvests.

"This is important, and Parme is a master at chasing hail," says Tundup. "A *da kurim*, an exorcism by arrow, would be best. If Sara is not better tomorrow, we will go to Yang-tsher to consult the lamas."

Until then we had been simply travelers. Now suddenly we are forced into the reality of the Hidden Land. Everything is quickly organized. We will offer the *chang* and pay cash. Messengers are immediately sent to find the village archers.

I already have partaken in arrow contests in Charka and Nang Khong. I admired the archers' agility, and I laughed and drank with the others, but I was not aware of the event's stake or importance. Today, Sara's health is at stake.

Soon, 12 archers appear with their arrows and their bamboo bows. The men place two mud targets within 50 feet of each other. In the center they deposit a sheep's shoulder blade, symbolizing the demon's heart. Before starting, the men sit cross-legged, their arrows in front of them, and sip chang while gossiping. Three butterballs are deposited on the cups' edges as a good omen. A scent of incense fills the air. Soon Tundup invokes the protective divinities and Guesar de Ling, the war king, so that they may guide the archers' arms.

"It is not enough to be skilled. We also need the gods," Tundup had told me. Barley is offered to the divinities, but now it is the archers' turn. "*Dering Sara kurim yinnnn!*—Today it is Sara's exorcism!"

The combat against the demons is savage. The long braids that the archers have rolled around their heads are unwrapped and fall onto their backs. "*Lhaaa Gyalooo! Kiii! Sooo! Tat!*" The gods are evoked. War cries, shouts of joy and rage echo in the valley. They are very good archers. Old Karma with his toothless smile and unbridled energy lets his instinct guide his arrow. But Sonam Chopel aims with great concentration, sticking his tongue out each time. Tundup is poised and dignified, but he is the first to laugh at his clumsiness.

When a dart strikes the heart of the lhu, they all group around the winner. "*Sooo! Sooo! Sooo! Kye ihasooo! Yul ihasooo! Ta ihasooo!*— Glory to the gods of my birth! Glory to the gods of the village! Glory to our protector!" they shout, and place grass on the winner's head.

The winner remains silent, his eyes closed, his face turned toward the sky, and thanks the gods. The chang flows freely, and everybody is taken by the wild game. The two groups of archers goad each other. The first one reaching 15 points wins. Chime Renzing's wife, Kunsang, is there, a hand over her swollen jaw. At the end of the whole affair, after the demon's heart has been pierced countless times, she timidly asks me if the archers could play for her.

For the future winner, she offers a long awl, which is indispensable for any caravanner. The tournament continues, this time to heal Kunsang's toothache.

Sara is not delirious this night. She is still asleep when Tundup comes to see us. "We can go to the Yang-tsher Monastery after having eaten," he whispers. Perhaps it is not necessary, but he insists. Tsering Tashi, the master of the ritual, is one of his friends, and he knows that the master could arrange a grand exorcism for Sara.

Lakpa, our Sherpa companion, and Karma Chodzom, Tundup's wife, will watch over our two daughters. Karma has already prepared the food for the route, a pile of doughnuts fried in butter. Sara is happy that she need not move.

Four hours later we arrive in Yang-tsher, one of Dolpo's oldest monasteries. Eleven great white-and-ocher chortens stand against the blond cliff's rocks. Its name, the "Island of Light," its size, and its majesty reveal its importance in Dolpo's history.

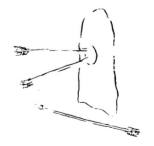

We enter the temple's great dark hall. As Tundup had predicted, all of Dolpo's monks are there, excluding the hail chasers. For the past two weeks, three lamas, fifteen monks and half a dozen assistants have prepared the *mendrup*, a ritual honoring remedies and medicinal herbs. Hundreds of ingredients—coming sometimes from very far—are dried, cut up, crushed, cooked, left to ferment, dried again, reground, mixed, soaked, and dried a last time. The ingredients are minerals, vegetables, wild yak blood, bear spleen, vulture gizzard, elephant mucus, cliff tar, and many other things. This mixture is finally turned into little irregular granules that heal all sicknesses. Mendrup is the universal remedy.

Drums and cymbals accompany the prayers of the religious ceremony, asking the gods for their blessing. The participants all have swollen eyes; their gestures are slow and imprecise, and their

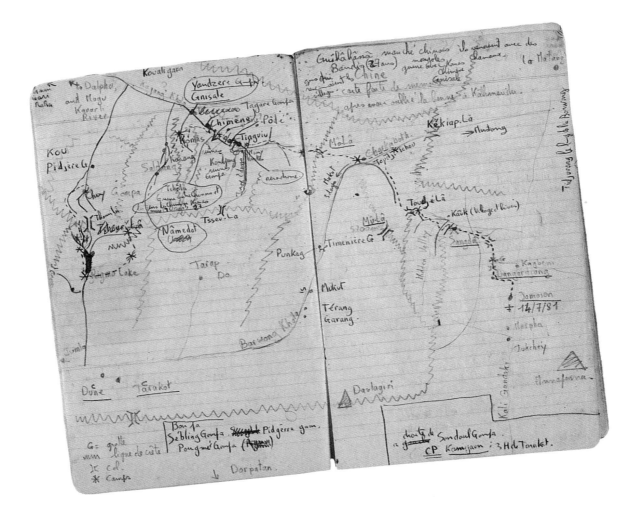

A mother and daughter eye us curiously as we stand in the tent. The mother wears totcha, a makeup made from a mixture of roots, to protect her eyes from the reflection of sun on the snow.

speech confused. Is it fatigue or drunkenness? It's impossible to distinguish the two. These men have been busy day and night for two weeks. They sleep where they pray and prepare their remedy. The chang cup is in front of them, and three women constantly fill it. Their task is to nourish and serve refreshments to the monks, who are not allowed to leave the monastery during the ceremonies.

We offer Tsering Tashi a tea brick and cash for the monastery wrapped in a silk scarf. Tundup explains Sara's sickness and the result of his divination. The man is tall and strong, his short hair is curly. The left side of his thick face reminds me of scary masks on the temple's pillars, because he has so many scars. His voice is deep, his large round eyes seem to look beyond us. He slowly nods his head. "That is what is thought," Tundup tells me once we are outside. "We arrived on time; the exorcism can take place tomorrow."

During every festival celebrating the middle of the summer, he tells me, an important kurim is organized by Dolpo's great lamas, during which the demons responsible for adversity, sickness, insects, and drought menacing the harvests are pacified. From the monastery at Yang-tsher, benefits flow all over Dolpo, but it is better to be present.

I suddenly understand Tundup's insistence on coming here. During the kurim ritual, Guru Rimpoche is once again invoked. He abandons his peaceful appearance of a wise Indian and takes on the angered form of Guru Drakpo, the miracle worker who subjugates the demons. His blood-red head is crowned with skulls, a third eye pops out of his forehead, flames stream out of his eye sockets, and his mouth reveals tiger teeth. He dances with five acolytes brandishing the *phurba*, the magical dagger. The dancers' long sleeves, ample dresses, and yak tails covering the scary masks flow in the wind.

The negative forces are exorcised by the ritual's power, the offering, chants, cymbals, and drums. Their effigy is drawn on paper and will be thrown into the flames. Before returning to Saldang, Tundup makes sure that a small package of mendrup is sent to Sara.

Two days later, Sara feels better. The worst of the hepatitis, which she likely got in Kathmandu, has passed. She asks to ride the pony.

We are here in the heart of Buddhist territory. Yet the whirlwind of ceremonies we took part in has very little in common with Buddha's original teachings. When Guru Rimpoche brought Buddhism from India to Tibet, the new religion had to mix with all the popular beliefs. Buddhism integrated the pantheon of the local gods and demons of Bon, Tibet's native religion. Transformed by Buddhism, these divinities, who had always been anchored in the nomadic tribes' imagination, never disappeared.

Thus we had seen them surface again. We could still read their power on the spectators' faces. These gods and demons mirror this country. They are savage, magnificent, and frightful.

Tilen pulls the Tibetan pony which carries Sara.

(pages 32-33)
Yang-tsher Gompa.

HEROIC SONG OF GUESAR DE LING

CONFRONTING HIS ADVERSARY IN A BOW DUEL:

"This song is the last one you will ever hear.

Vulture, perhaps you can escape to the sky,

Smile, disappear into the dust;

But you are a man, your heart is anguished.

My bow was given me by the gods to destroy evil.

It is made of a wild yak's rib,

kyang:
Tibetan wild donkey

Its string is made of *kyang* leather;

On my right side, the quiver is made of tiger skin;

The arrow is not from here,

The bamboo comes from the valleys of the south,

the iron of its tip from the north;

The feathers were given me by the Vulture King."

Monks and lamas
exorcise demons.

(pages 36-37)
A worshiper turns
his prayer mill
inside the large
monastery hall.

(pages 38-39)
Guru Drakpo and
his acolytes dance
around the fire
where the demon's
effigy is destroyed.

(pages 40-41)
Two horsemen pass
near the Changdzo
chorten near
Tinkyu.

Chu Gyen or the Distribution of Water

Gods and demons are implicated in all aspects of Dolpo's life and reign over Dolpo. The rite of Saldang, Saldang-Chu-Mendang—abundance of land, rarity of water—is witness to this effect.

Here, on the highest land of the Tibetan Plateau, the Himalaya blocks the monsoon rains. Nothing grows without irrigation. Fifteen reservoirs have been dug into the arid soil, so *chu*—water—can be gathered from the springs above the village.

In April, just before the plowing, precious water must be distributed among the villagers. Tundup then changes his role. Formerly amchi, he now becomes *tsipa*, the chief of Saldang's lower village.

The village of Shuk-tsher Gompa and its barley fields, a tiny oasis in the midst of the mountains (14,100 feet).

We assemble in his house's courtyard. The chang is there, the chang is always there. And once again the gods are invoked for *chu gyen*, the distribution of water. The rules are as old as the village itself. All the villagers sit in a circle. In front of each lies a stone symbolizing his house. A scribe near Tundup writes down the results.

The villagers of
Saldang distribute
water rights while
sitting around
Tundup.

"*Surkhang!*" shouts Tundup, first calling the name of Renzing Dorje's house.

The participants' eyes anxiously follow Tundup's hand, which throws two big dice made of barley flour. A five. Tundup places five small stones in front of Renzing Dorje. He calls a house name each time he throws his dice. Nobody discusses the results. Tundup is the chief, and the gods decide on the lot of everybody. Renzing Dorje knows that a five means that most likely he will be one of the last to receive water. He shrugs his shoulders and philosophizes: "The next time I will win. Everything balances out over time."

But water is so precious and the situation so desperate that there are often violent disputes during distribution.

"The rules of life must be very strict here," says Tundup.

After the sowing, animals are forbidden within the limits of the village, since they could eat the young shoots. If, during this time, a yak, horse, or goat is seen crossing a field, its owner must pay a fine of one measure of barley per footprint. If the animal has eaten part of the crop, Tundup is in charge of evaluating the amount of compensation. Even Tundup has to ask the neighbor's permission to leave one of his sick goats in the house's courtyard. Although these verbal rules are strictly followed—and in spite of the gods' intervention—Dolpo's land only produces five to six months of food per year and cannot feed its people. So the Dolpo-pa must search on the caravan trails for the food they desperately need to survive.

Excerpt from the sketchbook of a 15th-century Tibetan painter.

(pages 48-49) The first scanty precipitation falls at the beginning of the monsoon at the end of June in Saldang.

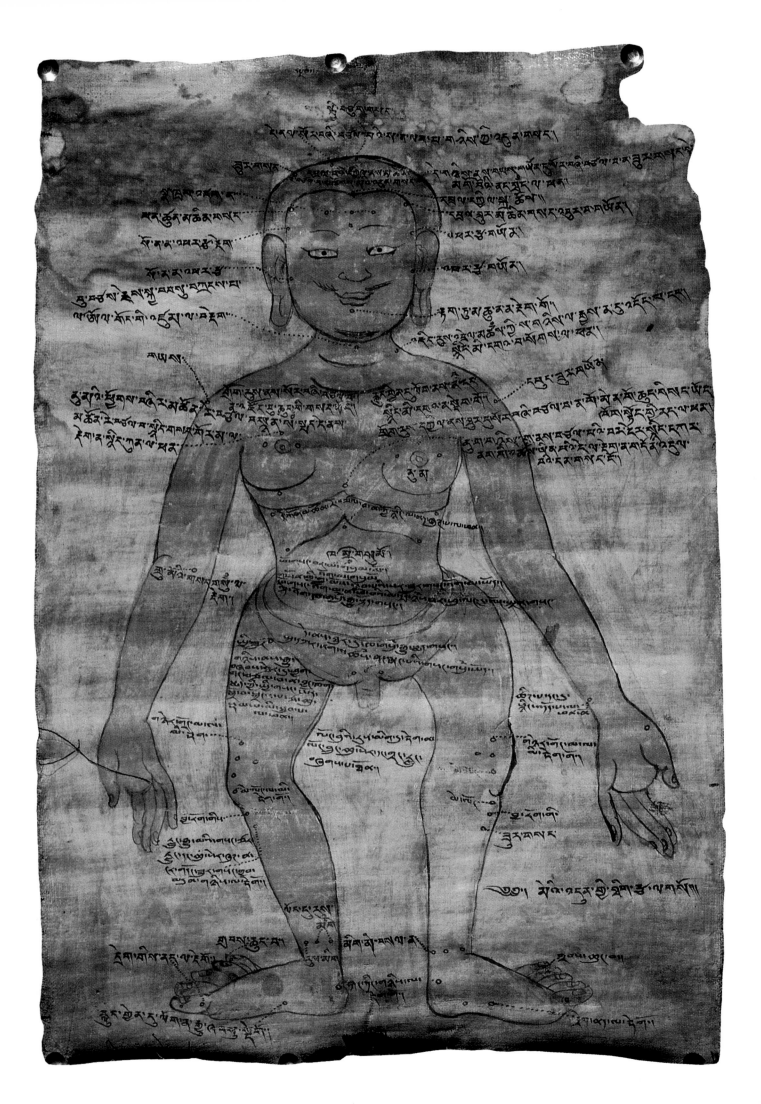

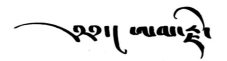

The Amchi

Labrang Tundup, the amchi, always starts the day with a short prayer, which he recites to the slow rhythm of a big drum hanging from his private chapel's ceiling.

The echo reverberates in the valley, as if to remind the protective divinities not to forget this handful of people, who obstinately survive in one of earth's most inhospitable regions.

All is silent next door in the room that serves as a kitchen, consultation office, and living quarters. One only hears the boiling water in the teapot sitting on the fire of yak dung.

On one side there are bookshelves, cabinets for kitchen utensils, and oil lamps. In a corner is a large prayer mill that Tundup, sitting to the right of the fireplace, activates with a leather strap. Against a wall is an enormous wooden chest made with a hatchet and filled with material, blankets, chubas, and sheepskin coats.

Drawing of a Tibetan medicine manual showing the placement of fire tips.

A man limps into the chapel and sits apart in the smoky room. The visitor comes from Namdo, a village located a half-day's hike from here. His pony had thrown him, and he has a terrible backache. As soon as he sees Tundup, he takes a heavy object out of his tunic, a kind of large stone covered with black fur. The amchi places it on a shelf and asks the man to step closer. He lifts up the man's sleeve, looks for a pulse, and closes his eyes. Then he makes a mo, or divination, and three times the dice clang in the cup.

After examining the wounded man, Tundup turns to me:

"I prefer that my patients not talk. Very often, there is a difference between what they say and what the real problem is. By observing their eyes, tongue, and pulse, I know what's really going on. Furthermore, the best way to know somebody is not to listen to them speak, but to see what they do."

Tundup then asks his son Tsering to fetch the blacksmith. Karma Chodzom, his wife, pours boiling tea into a wooden churn and adds a few crystals of gray salt. With a broad-bladed knife she cuts off one of the tips of the strange, furry stone brought by the visitor. The leather opens and reveals a pat of butter. She cuts a large piece off and throws it into the tea. She then wipes her greasy hand through her black hair and moves the churn's piston in a concert of gurgling.

We drink many cups of this invigorating beverage before going into the courtyard, where Tundup's red horse is tethered, and the blacksmith has already lit a fire.

The blacksmith plunges the tip of a long metallic rod into the fire of live coals. The amchi goes to his patient, who is sitting bare-chested. He slowly moves his thumbs across the spine, takes mysterious measurements, locates invisible reference points, and finally, with the help of a charcoal piece, draws six black dots on his patient's back and three more dots on his solar plexus.

Labrang Tundup treats a patient in his courtyard.

The amchi then throws a handful of juniper onto the burning charcoal and recites a short prayer, while the smell rises.

Two men immobilize the patient by his shoulders. Tundup takes the iron rod with a firm hand and applies the incandescent tip to the black marks. The wounded man groans, his muscles stretch, and his skin sizzles and smokes. The operation takes less than a minute. Nine small pink scars, the size of a shirt button, remain on the leathery skin. The exhausted man breathes loudly. Then, with a forced smile, he looks around him, gets up, thanks the amchi, and limps away, leaning toward the left.

Labrang Tundup is one of the first who felt our passion for Dolpo and its traditions. We have become something like his pupils. The more I learn about him, the more I admire him. Labrang Tundup is a master. He never has to raise his voice to get someone to listen to him.

(pages 54-55) Diane writes in her journal while a Dolpo-pa eyes her curiously.

tulku:
reincarnated,
very high lama

He is respectful, patient, and so polite that he sometimes appears shy. He comes from an aristocratic family related to the former *tulku* at Shey. His father lived there and was known for his wisdom and mastery of Tibetan medicine. Saldang needed such a man.

The villagers offered him the village's most spacious house— Labrang. The residence is a large, square, massive building with two stories and is larger at the base than at the summit. Having belonged to a lama, the house still has traces of red on its stone walls, which are intersected with rare and tiny openings. The roof is flat, and the juniper bushes piled on the terrace walls trail down the facade like the manes of shaggy horses. Notched trunks serve as ladders to climb to the next story. The planks are made of wood, and the inside walls are covered with dirt.

At our arrival, the amchi invites us to settle in the chapel. Labrang remains one of our favorite residences in Dolpo. When Tundup's father died, he remained seated in the meditative posture for almost five days. Then his body was transported to a crest for cremation.

The pyre burned without interruption for 14 days and 14 nights.

Small white balls, *kudong rinsil,* the indisputable signs of his great spirituality, were found in the ashes. Tundup carries some of them in a leather bag around his neck. The others were mixed with the ashes and clay and were made into a statue of Tara, the family's protective divinity. She is looking straight into our eyes from among the sacred books on a shelf.

The amchi tells me about the gods, demons, and their powers with as much conviction as when I had told him about faxes and television on the night on the terrace when he had asked me about the strange moving star I had called a satellite.

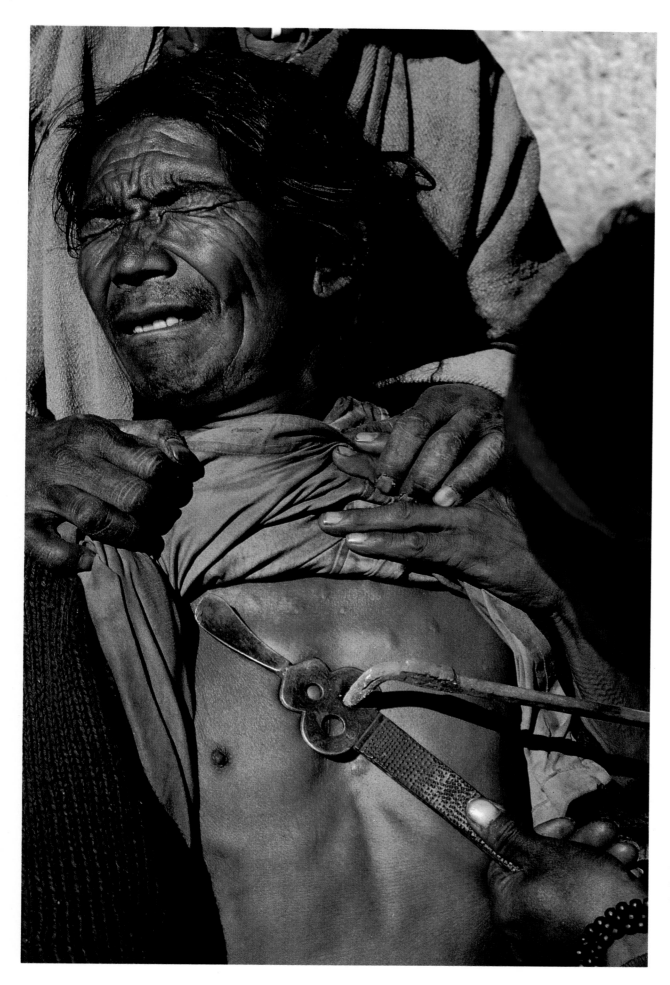

The mo, *a treatment with fire tips.*

(pages 58-59)
The village of Shuk-tsher on top of a cliff. Its name means "juniper thorn."

ཀྱི། བ་གར།

The Blacksmith

I often run into the *gara*, who transports his forge from one end of the village to the other. He repairs plowshares and spades, sharpens knives and sickles, and fills in holes in teakettles and pots. He is fed in every house and offered as many cups of chang as he can drink and sometimes a bit of grain, which he takes home. But only after the harvesting is finished does he receive his real salary for taking care of the tools necessary to the village life. With a backpack, he goes from door to door asking for his dues, and every villager gives him the quantity of grain he merits.

He is paid per job when he forges new tools or makes silver jewelry for marriages. This noble and delicate work enables him to be particularly well treated. He is given a tent in the courtyard, entrusted with precious metal, and is compensated with a generous salary paid in cash or with merchandise. He is fed as much as he needs and is given meat and the house's best chang. What emerges from his hands symbolizes a family's richness, and thus its power.

gara:
blacksmith

Plowing during the month of April.

Yet the garas, always in contact with metal, are considered impure in the Tibetan culture and are the lowest on their social ladder. Until recently they could not enter the houses of other clans.

But speaking of Dolpo, Tundup exclaims: "What would we do without the gara, on this heap of stones that devours plowshares every year?"

Yes, the blacksmiths are very useful. And I witnessed the amazing extent of their role.

In November the animals are killed for meat, which, at this time of year, is preserved for a long time by the cold. Tundup has called the gara. The gara is the only one who can take life. A yak waits patiently in the courtyard. The yak's legs are rapidly tied. The long rope immobilizing his hind legs is passed behind one of his horns. The animal's head is thus lowered and immobilized at the gara's boot level. It cannot move any more. Another strap is then rolled several times around its muzzle. The yak teeters into death without fighting, suffocated, its eyes wide open as if surprised.

Tundup and his 14-year-old son recite the text that guarantees a better reincarnation for the animal and erases the ill-fated consequences of its being put to death this way. Tibetan Buddhism has adapted to the necessities of daily life.

The gara, his eyes clouded with too much chang, works with great precision. The animal lies on its back and is cut up. Soon its skin is stretched on the ground, and a large bloodstain surrounds the carcass. Attracted by the spectacle and the smell, dogs keep returning, although they are chased away with stones. Neighbors and friends have come to help. The men are active, silent, diligent, and efficient. Children with runny noses stare wide-eyed.

While the meat is being cut up, the image of death gives way to

anticipation of the upcoming feast. The atmosphere relaxes. Tsering,

the son of the house, has put away his prayer book. He helps the butcher

fill the cleaned intestines with a mixture of blood, fat, meat pieces, and

tsampa.

tsampa:
**roasted, ground
barley**

*The blacksmith
and his assistant
come to suffocate
the yak.*

Tundup sits next to me and with his chin points to the gara, whose

forearms are immersed in blood:

"You know," he tells me, "he is also the father of my son Tsering."

I look at him, disconcerted.

"My first four children died. A girl survived, then a boy, but he was

fragile," continues Tundup, while looking at Tsering with affection.

"The demons had already taken four children from us. We attract them.

They pick on people with knowledge and rich people while they leave

the poor and those from the inferior clans alone."

Tsering, several days old, was given to the blacksmith for one day, according to the custom in such cases. That day, the gara changed the name of the infant and chose a name from his clan, symbolically accepting him into the low-caste family. He fed him and made tiny blacksmith tools, which the child would wear as a necklace for several years. That evening, the baby returned to the house of his legitimate parents, and the evil forces, confounded by the ruse, forgot about him.

"What demon would have wanted to take on the child of an inferior clan?" adds Tundup. "They already have so many problems!"

The sausage is thrown into a large pot of boiling water. The gara takes a long, curved needle from his chuba and pierces the intestines before the water boils. The children play in the spouts of blood shooting over them each time the needle makes a hole. The yak is now only a mass of

red meat piled on its own skin. The women bring the chang. Taking advantage of the relaxed atmosphere and the men's euphoria, the dogs become bolder and lap up the blood-impregnated earth.

Tundup discreetly evaluates the importance of every guest and offers everybody a different-size piece of sausage. All joyously accept their lot, with their palms stretched out. We eat voraciously, speak, laugh with open mouths, our lips and hands shining with juice and fat.

In the evening, the meat is piled on the terrace. It will freeze during the night, covered by the animal's skin. It will be preserved for more than a year and be frozen and dried over and over again.

It is time for the blacksmith to go home, carrying his part of the feast on his back: the yak's head, four hooves, and some internal organs.

Bending under the load, he passes through the narrow courtyard door and the horns catch. Tundup follows him and clandestinely slides three sausages into his pocket.

The silhouette with two heads slowly descends toward its house and disappears into the dark.

*The blacksmith
and his payment,
which he will make
into a stew.*

The Hermits

Often I stop. I look at the landscape that always makes my heart beat faster. What splendor! What majesty! One question continues to trouble me: How could people have decided to live here?

I often think about the classic theory that these people were chased away by some kind of invasion and came to take refuge in the mountains. I have heard of the king of the city of *Lho Mantang* who sent his four sons searching for new territories. Labrang Tundup told me the legend of the monkey and the mountain ogress whose union was the origin of the Tibetan people.

Lho Mantang: capital of the small kingdom of Mustang

"But how could people have decided to live here? It happened hundreds or thousands of years ago. There must have been better places to settle!"

Tundup and I sit on top of a ridge. Tired, cold, and thirsty, we contemplate this chaotic universe of rocks, cliffs, gorges, and ocher escarpments mixed under the dark blue Himalayan sky.

Lama Reuzen Tsultrin with his rosary and prayer drum in Shimin.

Tundup chews a piece of the bitter buckwheat pancake we are

sharing. Far down at the bottom of the canyon, a tiny green dot inside an ocher field is the only sign of human presence.

"Who would have wanted to settle here?" murmurs my companion, his eyes staring vaguely ahead. "Dolpo was chosen because it is in fact a savage area, inhospitable and solitary. One day, hermits must have been attracted by these mountains."

Tundup then tells me of the caves where the ascetics lived. On the way down to Saldang, he speaks about the wisdom and power of these men who spent years alone, meditating. Their reputation grew and attracted disciples. Little by little, other hermitages were built, then a monastery, a hamlet, and a village.

"There was not one valley in Dolpo that did not resonate with prayer drums."

Tundup quoted Sonam Lodro, whose disciples built Yang-tsher Gompa. He told me the story of Tsonga Renzing, who, from the summit of the Nien Pass, shot an arrow and vowed to settle where it landed. He found the arrow very far away at the bottom of the valley. The arrow had killed a rat, the incarnation of a demon. On this spot he built the first hermitage, called Chopa Lhakhang. Several years later the disciples built another one called Khang-Nyi, which means the second house.

"That is where you will live when you stay in Phiger," Tundup tells me. Also, the name of the village means dead rat.

Born on this arid land, the Dolpo-pa learned to take advantage of their region's strategic location. Their land is located between the great northern salt lakes and the fertile grain valleys of the south. Their yak caravans thus combed the mountains.

The monasteries, which had always played an important

commercial role in Tibet, grew bigger, as did the villages. At the heart of the caravan route, Dolpo flourished and acquired the reputation for being a source of faith and abundance, producing great men.

Tundup and I never failed to explore the ancient hermitages located in the cliffs surrounding the villages. Margom, where Sonam Lodro meditated, Gamoche, where Druptob Sangye Yeshe multiplied the grain, Reling, and Tegyam. The trails leading there are difficult, and more than once I had to use a rope. I always discovered in these caves traces of human presence and religious writings on the walls.

"Some of the men," says Tundup, "could cross the sky like a vulture. Others had the gift of prophecy or ubiquity."

Perhaps I smile incredulously. My companion continues with indulgence: "Think about all the energy you use to make this book, earn a living, and build a house. Imagine these hermits using as much energy to acquire true wisdom, an understanding of nature and of the world. Could you not conceive that they might be able to do so, just as you are able to attain the goal you have set for yourself?"

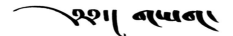

Yaks

Tilen Lhundrup's solitary house rests on a dominant shoulder of the Nang Khong Valley. When we approach, his dog, a Tibetan mastiff, barks furiously at the end of its chain. Tilen comes out and places his hand over the animal's eyes. It calms down immediately.

"Okpia me te!—I hope you did not have any difficulties!"

It is always difficult to go from the bright light outside into the obscurity of a Dolpo house. It is best to follow closely the master of the house, but sometimes you get lost. You then have to hold your arms in front of you to avoid bumping into a pillar, a heap of dried yak dung, a wall of salt sacks, or a pile of saddles and ropes. Finally, my groping hand finds a tree-trunk ladder. The notches are smooth from generations of feet wearing boots with yak-leather soles.

I climb toward the kitchen's pale blue light. At the height of a man, the smoke is so dense that I cannot stand without crying. I sit down with my legs crossed on a carpet to the right of the fireplace. A ray of oblique light descends from the chimney hole, where smoke clouds

Yak battle.

The Lhu

With one month's supplies, Karma, Lhakpa, and I leave, prepared to meet with winter. We depart Jumla on November 20 and, walking along the Jakdula *khola*, are on our way to Kagmara La and northern Dolpo. The season is well advanced, and the caravans are already heading south for the land of grain.

khola:
river, in Nepali

We often have to leave the narrow road so long lines of yaks can pass by. Our loads are heavy. We walk against the flow of hundreds of tired and slow animals.

I walk behind Karma. He sings a soothing nomadic song to the yaks. He walks regularly, bowed under the weight of a *doko*—more than 60 pounds. The animals do not bother him. Since he knows this region very well, perhaps he already imagines our camp, which will be located at the forest's upper limit. Perhaps he is also thinking about tomorrow's midday crossing of Kagmara. There is snow up there, but thousands of hooves have already dug the trail.

doko:
a basket that is
carried with a
front strap

Dawa, a young
porter from Darap.

When we pass the yaks, they press closely together along the trail's left side. Other yaks are more nervous and stop, then with surprising agility and rapidity suddenly gallop away to join the others. Their long curved horns pass a few inches from our chests. Their winter coat is long, thick, and shiny, and ripples with their movements. The *yak-pa* can only exchange a few words with us because they are swept away by the animal flow.

yak-pa:
a yak herder

"Yes, Tilen must be two days behind."

Suddenly, a man far ahead of us shouts and gestures. We can barely distinguish him from the yaks and dust. His voice is muffled by hammering hoofs, rolling rocks, yak breath, and creaking saddles and ropes. I stop. The man lifts his hands to the sky and shouts again. Karma does not hear him. An animal with golden fur stops, petrified, in front of Karma. Bent under his load and unaware of the danger, Karma continues to advance....

The first time I had met Karma he greeted me timidly by sticking out his tongue, as is the custom in Tibet. This was more than a year ago in Jumla. He had fled the Chinese invasion in 1959 and lived with his wife and three children in a dark and dirty room. He is small and thin. He is called Karma Chung Chung, "Little Karma." He is the only one who recently cut his hair in a crewcut. I was looking for a porter. He told me about all the trails he had hiked, and about his life as a yak-pa on the high Tibetan plateau.

No, he had never traveled with foreigners before, but he knew all the caves and shelters in case of danger. He knew all the passes. He knew every inhabitant of Dolpo, and he wanted to come with us more than anything. I thus had chosen the first porter I had met.

On the trail, seeing him always busy, bringing dead wood or yak dung for the fire, mending a tear in the tent, cooking a *chakpa*,

chakpa:
stew

combing a village for radishes, potatoes, or eggs, I understood why he had begged me to come along. Like me, his heart beats stronger when he is in the mountains.

The flow of animals stops behind the golden yak. With a quick, elegant movement somewhat resembling a dance step, the yak lunges at Karma. It plunges a horn into the chest of my companion, hurling the bent-over man and his load into the air like a bundle of straw. Karma is thrown onto the other side of the trail, while the frightened yak runs away. Karma lies on his back. His big open eyes do not seem to see anything. His face is fixed in an expression of astonishment. It is too late.

"No, not Karma!"

Nervous hooves pass close to us on the narrow trail. Two Tibetan boots stop. I look up.

The yak-pa shouts:

"I told you! *Yak tunga*! He is a goring animal!"

Karma's mouth is open, but no breath escapes. I am afraid to open his jacket and see the black hole the horn must have torn in his chest. I already hear the sinister gurgling of blood.

The closest hospital is four days' walk away, and what a hospital it is. There is nothing here, no possible help.

My heart beating, I open his clothes and search in vain for a hole. Long scratches cross his bluish chest, which moves slightly. He is

alive! Karma has several broken ribs. I am worried about the risk of internal hemorrhaging. His face deformed by the pain, he struggles for a breath that does not come.

I give him a cortisone injection to help him with the pain. Lhakpa goes to look for water to make cool compresses.

Karma and I are like two brothers. We have walked so much together! Since our last trip, he has believed that I would always be able to get us out of trouble.

It was last winter. Karma had never ventured into such deep snow. I opened the trail and sometimes sank into it up to my belt. When we reached a ledge just under a 16,000-foot pass, we decided to pitch our tent. Karma was terrified.

"Do not worry, I have clothes for all of you."

I distributed socks, overboots, gloves, hats, and down jackets. Karma's face immediately lit up:

"Now I will not die," he had said.

But now I am holding his two hands tightly in mine, and I am trying, like a shaman would, to infuse my strength into his inert body. Images tumble in my head of Karma always attentive at my side. I remember his vivacity and endurance, and the encouraging words he spoke, although he was afraid to cross a swollen torrent.

Now he lies there, folded in two, unable to breathe, his face waxen.

Another caravanner stops. These men live among horns, they must know something.

"What do you do in such a case?"

Standing very straight, his two legs spread apart, the top part of his *lopka* showing his muscled chest, he responds calmly:

lopka:
sheepskin coat

"Perhaps he will die, there is no amchi here."

They are used to the fragility of life in these mountains. It is the law of the strongest, the law of the most adaptable. I am out of place here. I am a naive foreigner who does not know the most elementary rules. I really should go back home.

The man has disappeared.

Evening falls and Lhakpa pitches the tent. Karma is still unable to walk. Sometimes he twists and groans. He cannot lie down, so we prop him in a corner against our backpacks. Several times during the night, I wake with a start to make sure he still breathes.

In the morning, without a word, he places his hand on my nape. He seems better. We return to the last village. What had taken us several hours of walking yesterday takes one whole day this time.

In the end of the afternoon we arrive in Hurikot, exhausted and starving.

ista:
exchange partner

The village is filled with caravanners. Renzing Dorje leads us into the house of his *ista*. We are filled with *rakshi*. Very quickly, the alcohol and fatigue plunge us into a state of bliss.

rakshi:
grain alcohol

Even Karma drinks more than his share of rakshi. I am so happy that he is still alive that I ask him every two minutes if he feels better. We sit on the terrace, taking advantage of the last rays of the sun. Finally I fall asleep, resting against a tobacco heap.

I wake in the middle of the night hearing the dry notes of a lute and frail voices of women. Steps rhythmically thump across the floor. The songs and rhythm accelerate. I decide to join the dancers when I hear Lhakpa's voice. Karma, wrapped in a cover, rests against a wall. The night is cold and clear, the sky full of stars.

This is one of those privileged moments when all barriers between people vanish. Rong-pa, Dolpo-pa, and Go Serpo dance together. We

sing and tell stories. While walking around the fire with a potato in my hand to represent earth, I try to explain the phenomena of days and nights, lunar cycles, the course of the sun, and the sun's position.

"The world's axis," they tell me, "is Mount Kailash, located several days' walking distance on the Tibetan Plateau. Tsewang will soon pass by here en route to the saintly mountain."

Before going to sleep, Karma and I speak of the bad luck we have had for the past few months; it has kept us from reaching Dolpo.

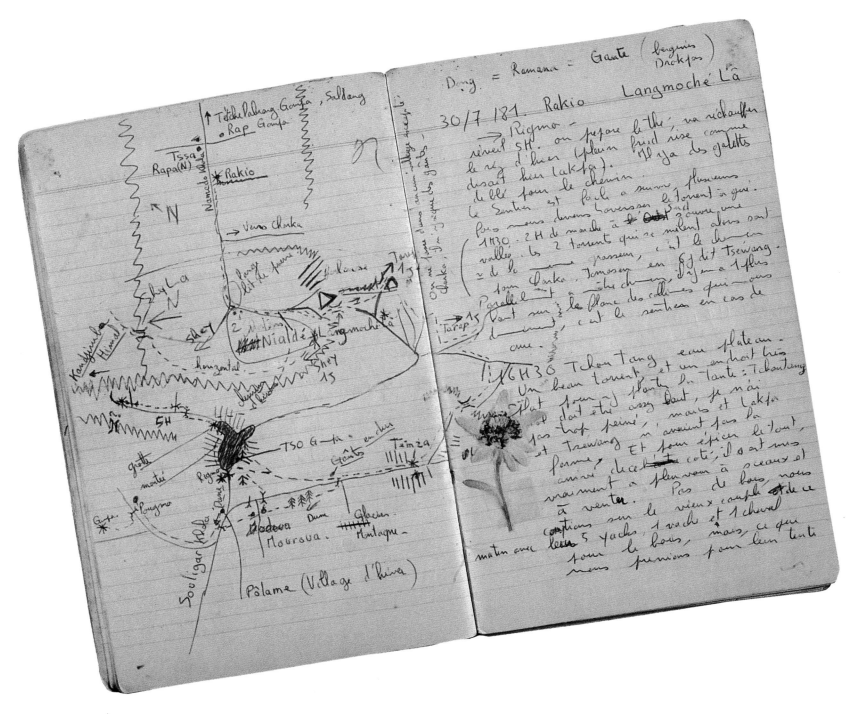

We were first stuck in the snow, then rebuffed by border guards, and yesterday there was this accident.

"We must discover the cause of these obstacles and ask the gods to help us. Perhaps we should consult with Tsewang before he leaves for his pilgrimage to Kailash," suggests Karma.

Two days later, I hire another porter, and we go to Naphakuna's residence. The *Rimpoche* knows my two companions and receives us warmly. He lives with his wife, children, mother, and a few servants in the monastery dominating the village. I look at the huts down below. They remind me of medieval villages in Europe, where peasants lived in the shadow of the castle and the church. A woman carrying wood comes out of the forest followed by her two children.

Happy to be alive, we are no longer in a hurry. And I know that we must settle our differences with the gods if we want to pursue our route to Dolpo. Lhakpa seems to take all this lightly, but I know that deep inside, like any good Sherpa, he also has doubts.

Tsewang's departure for Kailash approaches. The moment has come to speak seriously. The Rimpoche has heard about our situation. It is time to find a remedy.

Sitting close to the fireplace, the lama takes three little dice in his large hand and meditates silently for a moment. It is hot in the kitchen, and the lama wears only the left sleeve of his chuba, exposing part of his chest and right arm. A cat passes by and rubs its head against the Rimpoche's knee. The grandmother pours boiling tea into a churn and chases the chicken away with a kick of her foot.

The dice resound in the small metal box. The Rimpoche examines the oracle.

Two of his daughters come back from the forest and loudly unload

(pages 86-87) Little Karma climbs the Kabre La (17,000 feet).

wood. They caress the cat, laugh, fill their cups with tsampa, and, with one lick, lap the dry flour between two long gulps of tea.

The Rimpoche throws his dice again several times. He takes a long, thin book wrapped in a piece of fabric from the bookshelf, throws the content of his cup into the fireplace, and asks for more hot tea. Signs similar to the Yi-Jing are written on the book's pages. It is the *mope*, the divination book. He reads to himself and gives us his verdict:

lhu:
**underworld
divinity**

"A *lhu* of the low valleys has been following you."

Karma is hanging on his every word. He suddenly remembers the cause of all the troubles. It was the day in Juma when he had inadvertently knocked three small bowls of holy water from a chapel's altar.

gyap shi:
**an exorcism
ceremony**

"We must have a *gyap shi*, adds the Rimpoche, "or the demon will continue to block your way."

We gather tsampa, butter, chang, and meat for the ritual offering. Aided by Lhakpa and Karma, the monks prepare the 400 *tormas*, which will be placed on the altar. The Rimpoche is busy with another more difficult task. He makes three human effigies with buckwheat dough and they begin to take shape. He looks at me from the corner of his eye while making the tallest of the three small statues. He adds a backpack to it and a hat with a large rim.

torma:
ritual cake offering

He then laughs:

"Yes, Sahab, it is you. And this one is Karma, and that is Lhakpa."

He gives us each a dough ball and asks us to add some spit, fibers from our clothes, and some hair. He then shows us how to roll this mixture between the palms of our hands, against the skin of our forearms, our neck, and our forehead to add some of our road dirt, our smell, and perhaps some of our vital energy. We give him the dough balls, which he sticks firmly onto our respective effigies. The ceremony finally takes place after three days of preparation.

gompa:
Buddhist temple or
monastery

Tormas and the small statues are placed on the altar of the *gompa*. We sit behind the monks in the great monastery hall. The prayers start.

The voices slowly build into a melodious hum and undulate to the drums' rhythm. The sound vibrates in the chest. The night's coldness seeps in between the pillars of the vast hall. The monks sit under the trembling light of the lamps, wrapped in thick blankets. A wooden cup of salted tea, topped by a silver lid, stands in front of each of them. The grand statues of Buddha, Guru Rimpoche, and Tchenrezi contemplate us from their pedestals.

Soon the drums' rhythm increases, and the sound of the conch fills the space, resembling that of a fog horn. The cymbals burst in with a thunderous noise. The Rimpoche's finger follows the prayer text. The chant becomes more intense. The stupefying smell of incense impregnates the air. The monks seem to be taken by invisible forces.

The rhythm decreases in the middle of the night. The voices still rise, deep and strident in turn, punctuated by the crystal sound of a bell. The finger still runs over pages of the text. A monk stops singing to drink a gulp of tea, and an old woman immediately refills his cup.

The large hall's walls have disappeared now, eaten away by semidarkness. The strange chant, interspersed with complaints, slowly dies.

The finger suddenly is immobilized. There is a last burst of cymbals and drums in the hall. It is silent.

The old woman offers us some chang. The three of us sit cross-legged facing the altar. The Rimpoche lifts the lid of his cup and drinks a big gulp. Soon the prayers start again, this time less intense. The monks are smiling. One whispers something into his neighbor's ear, who laughs. Finally Tsewang gets up and motions a young monk to follow him, carrying our three effigies on a plate.

They circle several times around us before going out, illuminated by a burning torch. I rise to accompany them, but Karma pulls me back down.

Thus the lhu was among us in the semidarkness of this great hall. The lamas had called him, attracting him by their offerings of chang and fresh meat. Seduced and confused by alcohol and prayers, invocations and flatteries, he had mistaken our effigies for us.

Right now he is following the effigies in the night. Tsewang and the young monk are taking them to toss into the stream. The current will carry them away forever.

Later on, the Rimpoche tells me that they do not use a simple effigy to scare away the demons for high dignitaries and rich people of Tibet, but that they use a real man. The petitioner would offer his clothes, horse, and part of his fortune to his "straw man." The man had to leave the village and take the lhu with him.

A yak caravan heads toward Baga La.

Rich but banished, he had to cross three passes and never come back.

The Daughter-in-Law

"For my son, I searched among the girls of Saldang, but I found none. I went to Namdo, where I did not find any girls either. I went to Do, Nyisal, and Shimin with no greater success. Let's not talk about Tinkyu! I even went to Poksumdo, but it was even worse there. I found her in Phiger. Yes, the women of Phiger are the best."

Thus speaks Tilen Lhundrup in his lonely house overlooking the valley. He is happy to see me and constantly shoves the *phuru* filled with *nyingu*, the heart of chang toward my lips.

phuru:
wooden cup

nyingu:
a clear, mild beverage made from the first squeezing of fermented barley

Soon I am as drunk as my companions. The monk who read the sacred scriptures for several days to bring good fortune to the house, plays the *dramien*. The three strings' delicate and harmonious sound contrasts with the men's deep voices. Tilen's wife, Pema Kandro, pours salted tea, brown sugar, granules of yak cheese, and a large dab of butter topped by a pyramid of tsampa into a Chinese porcelain cup. She knows that I like *pemar*. This food is offered in time of festivities and is delicately kneaded with the fingertips.

dramien:
a lute with three strings

pemar:
grilled barley flour, butter, salted tea, and brown sugar

Puti Ongmo and her two daughters in a yak-hair tent in the Shey pastures.

Pemar looks and tastes like the dough of my grandmother's pies.

I am invited to sit in the place of honor on the thick Tibetan carpet.

"I am not the Dalai Lama," I exclaim, laughing.

Tilen touches my chin with his fingertips affectionately, before once again offering me the nyingu cup. I barely drink three mouthfuls when Tilen takes the cup from my hands to fill it for Pema Kandro.

He returns to the subject of his conversation, his daughter-in-law Puti Ongmo: "There is only one problem with her. She has not yet given me a grandson. She has only had daughters, like you. But...it will come. Tell me, do you know how you make a son?"

He whispers his question in my ear and interrupts all the other conversations. Even the lutist is quieter. They await my reaction. I open my hands in a sign of ignorance.

"You make love with a hat on!" he says, and everybody laughs.

And the music, singing, and conversations continue.

Puti Ongmo is now in Shey where she takes care of the Tilen yaks. As in other years, she will remain all summer with her two daughters in these high pastures, while her husband goes into the low-lying southern valleys a second time to bring in the rest of the grain.

Last month we spent several days with her in her black tent. I understand why Tilen is so happy with his daughter-in-law. She is pretty and has common sense and a good sense of humor. She is a good worker. She also takes very good care of the yaks and likes them. The yaks mean much to Tilen and give him a purpose in life.

The day of our arrival, a baby yak died. Puti Ongmo cut it up. She sewed the baby yak's skin around a bunch of dried grass, after

dri:
a female yak

having powdered it with salt. The *dri* thinks it recognizes its baby and begins to lick the poor dummy. The animal thus continues to produce milk, which otherwise would have dried up. Puti Ongmo then collects the precious liquid and makes it into yogurt, butter, and cheese during the following night and day. She then leaves, searching for the other yaks, which have dispersed into the mountains during the night. She returns for the milking.

In the afternoon, Puti Ongmo places her loom in front of the tent near the playing children. The women of Phiger have the reputation of being the best weavers of Dolpo. But other tasks remain: taking care of the young animals, giving them salt, collecting and drying yak dung for the fire.

Yes, Tilen the patriarch has every reason to be proud of his daughter-in-law.

Six months pass. While crossing Baga La on the way to Saldang, I encounter Lama Nyima going south. In his vague Nepalese he brings me news of Dolpo. "Tilen's woman just passed away." Surprised, I ask for more detail.

"No, not Tilen's wife," he said, "the wife of his son."

"You mean Puti Ongmo? Tilen's daughter-in-law?"

"Yes, yes! The woman you often visited in Shey. I myself cut up her body to offer it to the vultures."

kurim:
an exorcism

Puti Ongmo became sick, and, in spite of the *kurim*, she died last month. The Phiger girl of whom the old caravanner was so proud was no more. She was 26 years old.

"It will take a long time to find another one like her," Lama Nyima added pensively.

(pages 96-97)
In traditional fashion, Paljor Tsering places goats head to tail to be milked.

Yarsa-Kumbu

One summer night I encountered Jamyang and his wife Tsering Palmo in the high pastures. They offered me the hospitality of their black tent, and we spent several days together talking about our countries. They were surprised when I told them that it surely would take more than a year to reach my own village on foot. Later they asked if I wished to gather the famous *yarsa-kumbu*, which means summer grass, winter insect—as Jamyang explained to me.

I had heard already about this strange half-insect, half-plant, but until then I had thought it was one of the countless fables fabricated by the abundant Tibetan imagination. I was wrong.

In the morning Tsering Palmo rises first, careful not to disturb Jamyang's sleep. She is wrapped in a chuba. Tsering Palmo is a large, solidly built woman. I rest on the other side of the tent and silently watch her busying herself. She first blows into the fire and then pushes her long black hair back, leaving a streak of soot on her cheek. She has a strong and luminous face. She looks at me in her

Cho-kyi spins wool. She wears a tik-pu, *a silver Tibetan headdress worn by married women.*

99

own way: timidly, but straight in the eye. She prepares the bitter buckwheat dough for the pancakes that she fries on a metal plate.

It is summertime. The landscape has changed from ocher to a pale green in the two weeks since the June rains. We are at over 15,000 feet in a small hollow where a stream gurgles through meadows sprinkled with multicolored flowers. The yaks punctuate the landscape with black dots.

The mountain summits stay powdered with fresh snow in spite of the season. The snow falls during the night and melts during the day, but one can often find some the following day. By the end of September, when harvesting has barely begun, the torrent's banks already begin to freeze. We are walking on a carpet of tender grass.

From time to time, Jamyang kneels on the ground, leans over, and scrutinizes the ground. He then stands up and advances slowly, attentively.

"I gathered many here last year, but…"

Once again he kneels, and his eyes sweep through the grass in front of him. "You see, you see!" he suddenly exclaims.

"Yes, I see grass, flowers…"

"No, look there," he says, pointing with his finger. "Look at this black stalk. It vibrates!"

I do not know if it vibrates, but I distinguish it from the other grass. Jamyang then uses the point of his knife to dig around the sinuous stalk. He delicately removes the earth around the root, rinses the plant in the stream, and shows me his find. It is a perennial, fat, slightly twisted plant. It is about six inches long, and its yellowish root is about one-third its total length. It resembles an insect, a kind of caterpillar. When I examine it closer I see the different rings, fine bristles on its back, tiny legs just underneath its head, its large eyes, and the black stalk sprouting out of its head. For the first time in my life, I hold an insect and a grass intermingled with each other.

Tsering Palmo is surprised by my excitement. What! The go serpo did not know of such a common thing!

In awe, I ask why this strange creature Tundup had told me about was so much in demand. "It is a tonic," Jamyang replies laconically.

When he returns from his tent he adds, while contemplating our find: "It gives one strength." Jamyang looks like a conspirator. He looks around him, making sure that we are alone. Tsering Palmo has gone to the animal pen to milk the goats and sheep.

My companion then raises his index finger between his crossed legs and murmurs while leaning toward me: "It is an aphrodisiac. You can eat it like this or cook it in milk. But the best way is to mix it with a sparrow head and the piss of a snow frog. It is such a strong mix that if you do not have a woman with you, you'll go crazy!"

During the meal, we speak about the incredible metamorphosis of this insect into a plant. We speak about reincarnation. A warm friendship slowly develops.

In September, I visit the couple's village. They had invited me to come see the harvesting. Tsering Palmo is sick. I give her antibiotics, and several days later she regains her customary energy and joy.

Tsering and Jamyang are not rich. Only three of the yaks in their pastures belong to them. Their field is small, but it is enough for a

childless couple. Their relationship is filled with complicity and tenderness, an emotion that is rarely seen among Tibetans. They enjoy laughing together.

One evening after dinner, Tsering Palmo tells us that she is well again and thanks me for it. She then—very naturally—invites me to spend the night with her.

"But, Jamyang?" I say somewhat taken aback.

"Do not worry," replies Jamyang calmly. "You can offer me the chang afterward!"

I had heard about the Tibetans' liberal attitude. I also know that adultery often and simply happens the way Jamyang just proposed it to me. During my stay at Dolpo, the village women often tartly teased me, with accompanying gestures, to illustrate the relationship they suspected between my height and the size of my penis.

I am touched by Tsering's spontaneity and the natural way in which she made her offer. I respect this woman. She is intelligent and pretty. I then remember her hand squeezing mine, her body leaning perhaps a bit more than necessary against mine when we had danced, her attentiveness and kindness toward me. We had developed a certain closeness, but I see her more as a sister than a lover.

Tsering Palmo sees my embarrassment and does not insist that evening. She renews her proposition on the following days, as if to make sure that I had fully understood her. She finally accepts my refusal with good humor. The three of us remain very good friends, as we would doubtless have done if I had responded to her advances.

When I pass through their village I always stay with them. Tsering Palmo never hesitates to joke about our love story, while Jamyang sits silently in the corner by the prayer wheel with a smile on his face.

SUMMER GRASS, WINTER INSECT

by Maureen DeCoursey

Have you ever asked yourself why the Tibetans are so robust and happy? An uncommon saprophyte might be the explanation.

Cordyceps sinensis is a parasitic mushroom of the Hippocraceae family whose secrets must still be unveiled. It is one of the morphological secrets of our world that continues to intrigue scientists and the seekers of bizarre occurrences. For Himalayan inhabitants, it is the occasion of a seasonal outing not to be missed.

The Tibetans call it the yarsa-kumbu—the summer grass, winter insect. The Nepalese call it *jivan booti*, the herb of life. It is typical of the central alpine Himalayan meadows, but it is otherwise only found between 13,000 and 14,500 feet in Tibet, India, Bhutan, and Nepal.

Its life cycle is not yet completely understood.

During the short interval between the beginning of spring and the rainy season, the eggs of an unidentified moth of the Lepidoptera family hatch into a multitude of larvae. The larvae feed on prairie grass while awaiting their future metamorphosis. But all the caterpillars do not have the same future. The *Cordyceps* spores, while searching for a host, are transported by the wind. They land on the heads of unfortunate caterpillars. Their mycelium quickly buries itself in the caterpillar's body, while the fungus pushes outward. The fungus then pushes straight out of the insect's head to the latter's great dismay. In this singular union, the plant and animal remain alive until they are found by eager gatherers or the fungus finally dries up the caterpillar by exhausting its vital energy. The fungus then settles into the soil, produces spores, and a new cycle begins.

Cordyceps sinensis is invisible from man's eye level. Experienced

yarsa-kumbu

gatherers search on hands and knees, ear to the ground, scrutinizing the ground, searching for these thin, bright yellow, fleshy, sinuous stalks, which vibrate as they point to the sky. These fungi are a powerful tonic when dried, ground up, and mixed with milk or honey. They are said to increase one's vigor, endurance, and libido. This concoction supposedly also has the same effect on yaks. The Chinese pay more than $250 per pound, since uncommon aphrodisiacs never leave them indifferent.

Cordyceps sinensis is actually recognized as an endangered species in the Nepalese Himalaya, because of excessive harvesting. It is now illegal to gather and export it for commercial purposes. Reports have shown that Tibet's traditional gathering areas have also become depleted. The aphrodisiac market being what it is, the black market continues to prosper, in spite of the above-mentioned measures.

(Maureen DeCoursey is currently researching the medicinal and aromatic plant market of the Himalaya. She is working with Yale University and the King Mahendra Trust for Nature Conservation in Kathmandu).

POLYANDRY

"Do you have a brother?"

"Yes."

"Does he sleep with your wife?" a young woman asks me, very naturally, without a trace of embarrassment. She is beautiful, with big almond-shaped eyes and high cheekbones. She has the mysterious beauty of an insect. Her bangs fall to her forehead and her freshly washed and braided hair shines with butter.

Without waiting for my response, she shifts her attention to her loom, where her hands arrange the long threads of yellow, red, and brown wool for a future blanket.

"No, no!" I respond.

Encouraged by her frankness, I ask her: "And you? Your husband has a brother, do you sleep with him?"

A young woman of Dolpo.

(pages 106-107) The black tents of the high summer pastures, where the dri, the female yaks, are kept with their young.

"Yes," she answers looking me straight in the eye.

"But...isn't your husband jealous?" I ask.

"No. He has a good heart," she replies.

When I tell this anecdote to Rakpie, a caravanner from Phiger, he tells me another story.

Gnichor Puti was the only daughter of the village's rich family. She had fallen in love with Tsewang, a good-looking and robust young man, but he was a Chogmi—a newcomer. In the eyes of Phiger's villagers, these men—who had settled in Phiger four generations ago—remained foreigners and were a separate group.

"Our mouths, our cups, our houses, and our hands are different," explained Rakpie. "The Chogmis cannot eat with us. We do not belong to the same world."

Gnichor Puti's father was therefore furious, but his daughter was deaf to his anger. She wanted to marry the man she loved, so she ran away with the Chogmi. Later, her parents forgave her because she was the family's only heir. And the marriage finally took place. The young couple moved into her parent's house. Tsewang gained the family's respect because of his righteousness and eagerness. But the herds were numerous, the lands vast, and the work so important that he asked his young brothers, Tenzing and Tarki, to come live with them. They soon expressed the wish to share the young woman, and this was naturally agreed to.

As far as the work was concerned, the tasks were fairly divided. While one of the younger brothers left for Tibet to search for salt, the oldest brother stayed home with the woman to take care of the harvests. The third brother spent the summer in the high pastures with the female yaks and their small ones.

Sometimes Gnichor Puti went to join the third brother to fetch butter. Sometimes she stayed five or six days under his black tent. When the caravanner returned from Tibet with the salt, he was offered the welcoming chang, the *dong chang*, which was started fermenting the day of his departure for his return. All three drank together. Then Tsewang discreetly left to spend a few days in a friend's house. The roles changed with the seasons and activities. The oldest, Tsewang, was officially the children's father. His younger brothers were considered uncles. The woman never stayed with two brothers at the same time. The herd, trade, and harvests prospered, and the number of children was limited naturally. Sometimes this system caused fights, but the family spirit always prevailed.

When Tenzing, the second brother, fell in love with another woman, he left to be with her. Several children were born from this new union, and the oldest son was offered to the two brothers and Gnichor Puti, who had had only daughters.

Rakpie's own life story is also interesting. Married to Pema, he spent more days roaming the mountains with his yaks than with his wife. Until the day Pema fell in love with another man. All three decided to live under the same roof. This arrangement has the suggestive name of *soum*, "eating triangle."

(pages 110-11)
The village of Kagar in the Tarap Valley and the yak caravans that return with Tibetan salt at the end of July.

(pages 112-13)
The house of a rich caravanner in Do in the Tarap Valley.

The Salt of Tibet

It is the end of June. The monsoon rains are late and the irrigation canals dry. Without its grass carpet and summer flowers, the landscape resembles a skeleton whose bare bones protrude from the arid soil.

In the distance, a long line of the faithful tours the fields. They are led by Parme Tuwa, the hail chaser and rainmaker. Bent under the weight of statues and religious books, they beg the heavens to send them the long-awaited water.

At Tawa, Tilen's house overlooks the Nang Khong Valley. A lama dressed in his monkish robe burns incense in a barley field, whispering prayers to protect the land from harmful insects. The lama is so absorbed in his meditation that he does not notice the family of bharals peacefully eating the young sprouts behind him.

The son of a caravanner settles down for the night protected from the wind by salt sacks.

Pema Ongmo sees them. Furious, she runs out of her house and throws stones. The bharals lift their heads and move away without haste, dignified, their gray-blue fur blending with the soil.

ཀོལ་པོ་ར་ཁ་ཡ་ག་ཁུ་རང་ནས་རྒྱ་ཆེན་པོ་གལ་བ་ངེད

ༀ རི་མོ་འདི་ཤེས་བསྐུར་བ་ཆེན་པོར་ཀུ་ལྦེབ

A slow whistling sound emerges from the other side of the valley. Pema Ongmo throws a last stone and crosses the field once again. A line of black dots advances from the north toward Tawa.

I distinguish the head of a golden yak, with a bright red yak tail tied on his forehead, the only bit of color in the landscape.

Tilen has returned with the salt from Tibet.

When he arrives, we bow respectfully before each other until our two foreheads touch, with our hands joined in front of our chests. We salute each other thus after long separations.

Tilen, his son, Karma, and their friend Lhundrup watch so that the yaks do not leave the narrow trail dividing the fields. Then the three men unload the animals facing the house.

fadse:
thick wool sacks in
which the yaks
carry grain or salt

The *fadse* fall heavily onto the ground. The breathless beasts tremble with fatigue and stand still. Tilen looks worn out, but his eyes shine. Without a word, he uses the brass hook hanging from this belt to open one of the sacks. Gray salt crystals emerge. Tilen plunges his hand into them with delight.

How many days has this salt traveled?

The Lake Drabye salt flats are located more than 150 miles away. The salt is collected on the edge of a seasonally flooded lake basin. The Drok-pa bring the salt near the Nepalese border. While hiking to the south, they must cross the Tsangpo (Brahmaputra) on the 12th day. The waters are too high, so the pack goats and sheep are left on

the northern bank. Only the yaks are strong enough to fight the current and swim across.

In Kyato Chongra, Tilen and the other caravanners from Saldang, Namdo, Komas, Gnisal, and Phiger come to meet them with their yaks loaded with corn and barley.

On the second day of their trip to the north, the Dolpo-pa cross the Tibetan border at the Khung La—the Khung Pass. They leave the mountain chaos behind them and penetrate the Chang Tang's vast land. They hike two more days, and then the caravanners see the Drok-pa tents on a grassy plain near a lake. This is where, as Tilen puts it, the "exchange of life" begins.

Before the Chinese invasion of Tibet, from generation to

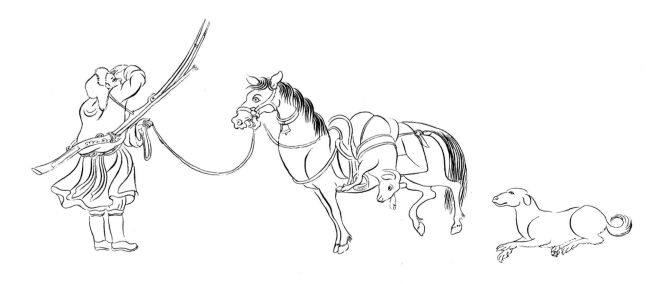

generation, every Dolpo-pa had a special partner among the Drok-pa with whom he could trustingly negotiate.

These traditional commercial ties were severed by the invading Chinese who, since 1959, have controlled the trans-Himalayan trade.

Since then, a representative from the government decides on the rates, quantities, and exchange partners.

The Chinese government thus determines the precise exchange date for every village.

The Dolpo-pa and Drok-pa now only have three days to conclude their transactions. These encounters used to be more than purely commercial and lasted a lot longer. All the restrictions have gradually weakened the ties that united the two communities.

Tilen Lhundrup in his surcoat.

Salt and grain are mainly exchanged, but the wool of the Chang

The threshing and sifting of barley in Shimin at the end of September.

Tang sheep is highly appreciated for its quality. So is the sheep's fat and dried meat.

(pages 122-23) Barley and buckwheat are put into heaps in Saldang.

The Dolpo-pa have trading in their blood. I was asked many times during our first encounter what I had to sell and what I had come to buy. I had simply come to "see" and "discover," but the Dolpo-pa do not understand this motivation. They always travel with a precise goal in mind.

A Dolpo-pa finally gave me an acceptable alternative: "If you have not come here to trade, you are on a pilgrimage."

From peregrinator I had become a pilgrim. Indeed, it was something like that. I was a pilgrim. It is the only other reason somebody could be motivated to venture to the Hidden Land.

Renzing Dorje

I like Renzing Dorje, with his square jaw, penetrating look, and the straight way he carries himself, his legs slightly spread, very dignified. I like the way he wears his *lopka*, which is open on his bare chest in the middle of winter. In fact, I like his virility.

lopka:
sheepskin coat

Renzing Dorje reminds me of the American Indians I never had a chance to meet.

I was thus very happy when he agreed to travel with us, driving four of his yaks before him to transport our loads.

At the end of our long tour, when the moment came to pay him for his work, the yak-pa asked me boldly for twice as much as we had agreed upon before leaving.

"Renzing Dorje! Yo koura tick chaina!—That is not right!" I protested. He was surprised by my spontaneous reaction to his deception. The brazen Renzing Dorje was disarmed. He smiled, took my hand, and without a word accepted the price we had originally negotiated. He had tried. After all, that was the first time that he had

Renzing Dorje puts a packsaddle on his yaks.

dealt with a go serpo. Later I heard that Renzing Dorje was known for his cunning.

Our story became very popular in Saldang. The people of Saldang appreciated the anecdote so much that even today they often exclaim, *"Renzing Dorje! Yo koura tick chaina!"* to relax the atmosphere when a dispute arises between two village inhabitants.

THE POSTMAN

Renzing and I became friends. A year later, we walk together, two moving dots on the gray, endless plain of Nyelde. We had thought we could reach Saldang that night, but the soft snow into which we sink up to our hips slows us down on the pass's northern side. The sun vanishes behind the ridges, and, as on every evening during the winter, the stream is covered by ice.

The legs of my wet pants begin to freeze. It feels as if I am walking in a cardboard box. I no longer feel my feet.

Renzing Dorje and I had left Ringmo two days before.

We had taken the lake trail in order to reach Saldang as quickly as possible. My companion would never have chosen this rarely used trail on his own. He would have crossed Baga La. This is the path travelers commonly take. We speak little while walking. I do not know what Renzing Dorje is thinking about. I am absorbing this incredible landscape. We have developed a silent complicity: a hand stretching out for a difficult passage, a smile of encouragement, a handful of dried fruit offered without a word. We are two men traveling through the mountains.

Before leaving Ringmo, our host prepared an imposing pile of wheat and buckwheat pancakes and several pounds of boiled potatoes roasted with salt, wild garlic, and red pepper. We, of course, brought the essential brick of Tibetan tea, the "horse of the solitary traveler," as the Dolpo-pa call it. The first day, we followed the trail sculpted into the cliff above the lake's west bank. It is sunny but windy. The clouds' shadows run straight across the water's surface toward the northeast, where we are heading.

We slept in a cave that is deserted this season, but which shelters Ringmo's shepherds during the summer. The next day we climbed the pathway on the northern side of the lake, which resembled a gigantic lapis lazuli set between the red cliffs. We spent the night under the stars at the foot of a big pine tree near a stream.

"This is where the wood comes from to build houses and bridges in northern Dolpo," says Renzing. The ground is covered with wood shavings left by loggers. Tonight they feed our fire and serve as an ideal mattress for our sleeping bags.

I like to travel without a porter. The weight on my back soon becomes an integral part of my body, and without it I would feel strangely incomplete. I carry the bare minimum in my pack: not even an extra pair of jeans. This is freedom.

We leave early in the morning and walk until nightfall. We push each other without a word, watching each other discreetly. On the second day, we once again see snow at the summit of the Chagar La pass. The crust no longer supports our weight at this time of the day. It breaks with a damp sound, and we sink into the snow. We stop for an instant. Is it the altitude, air quality, or the joy of having crossed the pass? We are both euphoric, as if we had just had a lot of chang. The landscape is untouched by the scars of roads or power lines. Only a trail's delicate line is chiseled into the mountainside. I cannot

see the villages from here, but I know them. They are made of clay and stone and blend almost invisibly into the landscape. One can barely glimpse the terraces' winding outlines surrounding them. Far down the north face we finally leave the snow behind. In Nyelde we begin to race against the night. We have half an hour to find shelter. Only the rolling pebbles under our feet disturb the plain's silence. After ten hours' hiking, my body still uses untapped energy. But if I stopped for only an instant, I would surely be unable to go on.

We must continue and find an overhang, with perhaps a bit of wood or dried dung left by travelers. We will light a fire, get undressed, and slide into our sleeping bags while the water heats for the tea.

chapka:
yak stew

Tomorrow we will reach Saldang, where Renzing Dorje's wife awaits us. She will prepare a rich, smelly *chapka* and quarts of buttered tea. I will dry my clothes and rest for two days, stretched on the terrace, dreaming in the sun, sheltered from the wind. In the four roof corners of the house, prayer flags will flap furiously, homages to the gods who will have enabled us to cross the mountains.

But right now I am walking like a well-oiled robot.

The landscape sinks into the night. Childhood memories pop into my head, a color, a movement, a face, without apparent logic. I remember the taste of hot chocolate at the Dalloyaus' house facing the Jardin du Luxembourg.

"Say, are you having an erection?"

Renzing Dorje has had enough. How long have we not said anything? During these past hours, we have walked next to each other, our legs moving in almost perfect synchronization. My energy concentrates solely on the quest for a nighttime shelter.

"What did you say?" I responded.

Lahkpa Gyalzen Sherpa, Tundup, and Eric Valli, wearing lopkas, are photographed in the village of Saldang.

"Do you have an erection?" He repeated.

"*What?*" I asked again.

"Yes! You made love to Diane so often in the tent," Renzing Dorje adds, remembering our first trip together. I look at him dumbstruck, before giving in to laughter, which infects my companion and echoes between the mountains. We are hysterical. One noise…a cough…we collect ourselves, short of breath, with shining eyes.

An old man stands before us, very straight. He has come from Namdo and is going to Ringmo. He is the postman. Very seriously, he shows me a small package of letters carefully wrapped in fabric sealed with resin. Then he carefully shoves the news from the Hidden Land close to his *phuru* in a pocket. He carries a rolled sheepskin surcoat in which he has food for a three-day hike. A dagger, a needle case, and a Tibetan tea brick hang from his belt.

phuru: traditional Tibetan wood cup

He shows us an overhang in a perpendicular valley, which we must reach before nightfall. I ask him to stay with us and share our dinner, but he knows a place several hours from here, he says, and he likes to walk in the moonlight.

The Shey Tulku

I had often heard about the Shey Tulku, who is considered a true saint in Dolpo. He lived in retreat for about ten years in a monastery at the foot of Shey, the Crystal Mountain.

The monastery of Tsakang belongs to the Kagyupa school, the spiritual descendants of the poet Milarepa. The monastery is built at the foot of an ocher cliff, from which it derives its name. It is surrounded by a fantastic array of gorges and mountains and always reminds me of pictures of the comic book character Tintin in Tibet.

They must have seen us from afar. The dog's barking echoes against the cliff. It had been locked in.

Pictures of Karmapa and the Dalai Lama, two great leaders of Tibetan Buddhism, sit on a dusty altar.

We wait in a sunny court. It is hot and all is still. A monk comes out of the gompa and brings us tea and tsampa. I offer him a *brick of tea* and some money rolled in a *khata,* a ceremonial scarf, and I explain that I would like to meet the Tulku. "He is in solitary meditation," answers the monk, before disappearing into the monastery.

brick of tea: Tibetan tea leaves are pressed into a brick, from which they are crumbled to make tea

On the other side of the wall I hear snippets of conversation. When

the monk returns, he tells me to wait in front of the door. It is a
double door, cut with a hatchet and probably brought from Tso long
ago. The panels are heavy and thick. They traversed the mountains
on yak backs. I had come across these caravans before, carrying
trunks, beams, and planks destined for use in building houses. The
scent of freshly cut wood trails the caravans in this sterile and often
odorless world. The trails are narrow, hilly, and winding. The pieces
of wood catch on rocks, and the yak-pa must be very vigilant. The
ropes slide and often cut the yaks' leather packsaddles, because of
the continuous jolting and the weight.

This door doubtless has a long history. It has opened and closed for
how many Tulkus? The sun illuminates the monastery's facade. The
paved courtyard is a furnace. I fall asleep sitting on the ground.

"Have you come to speak to me?"

The voice makes me jump. I open my eyes and see the still-closed
door, behind which is the Shey Tulku.

"Yes. I came here two years ago, but you did not receive anybody
at that time."

I tell him about my love for Dolpo and my travels.

"I would like to ask you for advice. I must make an important
choice, and I do not know what decision to make. I..."

"The details are of no importance. When two paths open in front of
you, if you are strong you choose the most difficult one, the path that
will demand the most of you."

The Tulku then adds, after a brief silence: "I have shoes that are
now old. Could you bring me some others when you return?"

"Of course, but I need to see them and measure them."

Creaking on its hinges, the door opens just enough for a used black shoe to pass through. His hand is large and solid with thick fingernails. His skin is dark and his veins protuberant. I find myself comparing this hand to the door separating us.

The monastic career of the 16th Shey Tulku started somewhat strangely in 1928. His predecessor had died of smallpox after wishing that in his next reincarnation he would be more dedicated to the Dolpo community and less inclined toward women than he had been.

Several years after his death, as dictated by tradition, the Karmapa, head of the Kagyupa school, saw by divination the precise signs that would help them find the new Tulku. He then wrote down this information in a letter. Lamas were sent to search for the new Tulku. They had to look east for a place called Drakhar, the white cliff. A willow and a spring were close to the house. A meadow was to the north.

The family was well-off. The father's name was Dorje and the mother's name Tsering. They had four daughters. One of them had crossed the pass to marry in another valley. The only boy's name was Sangye. He was to become the future representative of the Shey line and the one they had to find.

Several emissary groups were sent. They explored Panzang, Barbung, Sherpa (Kali Gandaki), Lho Mantang (Mustang), and even went to Tibet, but without success. There are many white cliffs in the Himalaya, many willows, passes, many people named Tsering and Dorje. Discouraged after three years of searching in vain, one of the emissaries went to the Tsurphu monastery near Lhasa, the headquarters of the Kagyupa school, to ask the Karmapa for more details. But he could give him no other information than what was already mentioned in the letter. He recommended perseverance and

(pages 134-35) Three generations are shown in this picture: the grandfather Lama Karma Tenzing (62 years old), his son Lama Norbu (22 years old, combing a Milarepa tanka, a religious banner), and his grandson Urgen (6 years old), asleep on his knees.

advised the envoys to take with them some common objects that had belonged to the 15th Tulku. He also added that the child had a scar on his cheek. The lamas began their search once again.

One day, near a white cliff, two envoys saw a house and a willow. A spring ran next to it, and to the north lay a grassy plain. In the courtyard a couple rested in the sun. The two lamas approached. They had come from afar and asked for something to eat. The woman prepared tea, and the religious men learned that the names of their hosts were Tsering and Dorje.

A group of children was playing a bit farther away in the fields. Encouraged after so many years of searching, the lamas told the parents about their real motivation.

The man answered curtly that the Tulku could not be here since he only had daughters. The woman brought the tea, and one of the envoys pulled a phuru from the pocket of his chuba. A child then approached and asked him what he was doing with his cup and why he wore his rosary around his wrist. The boy had a scar on his cheek. His name was Sangye. The father had lied because he didn't want to be separated from his only son.

The two lamas then bowed in front of their Tulku, for whom they had searched for four years. But the angry father chased them away.

"Take your cup, your rosary, they do not belong to us! Our son is not your Tulku!"

Only after two years of conflicts and the intervention of the highest authorities of Dolpo and Lho Mantang was the now eight-year-old child brought to Shey in a grand procession. The reigning lama began the chant: "Illuminating Dolpo, a sun rose from Drakhar…"

But the young Tulku turned out to be undisciplined and short-tempered. Following a dispute, he left Shey Gompa to study in Tibet.

After his initiation several years later, he returned a tall and strong man to Dolpo. He never took a wife as the 15th Tulku had wished. He remained in meditation for years. The Dolpo-pa brought food to the front of the monastery's door, and the Tulku came to fetch it when night had fallen. Then for about three months there was no sign of life at Tsakang Gompa. Afraid to disturb the lama's meditation, nobody dared to call him. Rumors spread across Dolpo that the Shey Tulku was dead. Men took turns observing the gompa. Finally, one day at sunset a shepherd saw a trail of smoke escaping the roof. Dolpo's heart began to beat again.

The Shey Tulku thus remained alone for nine years. Later, people came from all over to ask him for his blessing and advice. The sun that had risen on Drakhar went down during the winter of 1991. I heard about the Tulku's death, and I returned for a last visit.

He had been packed in salt in the meditative posture following the tradition for preserving the great lamas' bodies. Pilgrims gathered in front of the body, lit a lamp, and began to pray. Before leaving, they took with them a bit of the salt that had escaped from the bamboo mat containing the body. These precious crystals are said to have the power to heal.

Soon, other emissaries left with a letter in their bag, searching for the child into whom the 16th Shey Tulku had chosen to reincarnate.

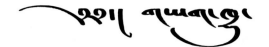

The Yak Caravan

From time to time, Tilen Lhundrup bends over quickly to gather a stone on the road, then throws it with an angry shout at a trailing yak that is blocking the yaks behind it.

The date of departure finally has arrived. All the caravans from Dolpo, Phiger, Gnisal, Komas, Shey, Lurri, Namdo, and Karang converge on the grain route. Over a period of ten days, more than 2,000 yaks, half of them loaded with salt, will cross the high passes. Tilen urges his 24 animals on. His wife, daughter Dawa, son Chewong, and their friend Lhundrup oversee the walk and round up stragglers. The caravan passes through Saldang in a cloud of dust and barking dogs. All along the way, men and women stop Tilen and offer him a cup of chang and buckwheat pancakes for the road and whisper in his ear a few orders for him to bring back. They will not go. Lacking pack animals or being too old, they remain here and watch over the almost empty village. They will live at a slower pace within the rhythm of a few winter religious ceremonies. Then the

Karma Tenzing, a young caravanner from Saldang.

melting snow and the arrival of spring will bring life back to the village, and the caravanners will return for the sowing.

The caravan passes the chorten, prayer wheels, and the monastery. Then it slowly climbs alongside the stream. Tilen is more peaceful now that the yaks have gotten into a rhythm. His hands behind his back, he stumbles over his long rosary at each step and murmurs the Chenrezig *mantra*, the mantra of the Great Compassionate One: *"Om Mani Padme Hum…Om Mani Padme Hum…Om Mani Padme Hum*—Oh, the jewel in the heart of the lotus."

mantra:
**a sacred sentence
that reportedly has
spiritual powers**

He walks a few steps ahead of me, his chuba's right sleeve hanging down his back. Not once does he look back at his village or his house. To avoid attracting demons, he was careful to let the fire in his house go out on its own. He is concentrating on his yaks and the trail.

"I know this trail," he once told me. "How many times have I hiked it? But so many things can happen…."

Last spring he had discovered the frozen bodies of a man and a child at the summit of the 16,000-foot Chagar La pass. The man lay under his lokpa, his eyes already eaten by the crows. The child's frozen body lay a bit farther along, under part of a blanket. The father and daughter had been surprised by a storm and had succumbed to the cold and exhaustion.

"What did you do with the bodies?" I had asked him.

"Why worry? Eaten by the vultures at the village or at a pass's summit, isn't it the same thing?"

Some years ago, Chime Renzing was surprised by an avalanche and lost three of his friends. He left last year for a pilgrimage to Mount Kailash where he thanked the gods for having spared him. Here, unforgiving nature leaves the people fervent and fatalistic.

Tilen had told me about his worries at the beginning of the winter. He had shown me the long clouds streaking the sky's dark blue, and we saw the bharals coming very early down the mountains, a sign that snow would be early this year.

Lhundrup has just loaded a yak with two sacks of salt. Each sack weighs more than 60 pounds.

"The animals know," said Tilen. The lamas were questioned and consulted their calendars, but they could not agree on a good departure date. They pushed back the date. They said that the omens were not favorable. Finally one morning the eagerly awaited shout resounded from roof to roof: "The lamas know, the lamas know!"

The caravan left Saldang on November 17, some 15 days later than in other years. The brooks were already frozen. Men's silhouettes were thicker with heavy lokpas, and the dried earth seemed to wait for the snow that would soon cover it and freeze-frame the lives of the handful of men, women, and children who stayed home.

In front of us, across the stream, a caravan that probably came from Komas reaches a crest. Another one, probably the caravan we had seen getting ready when leaving Saldang, advances slowly behind us. I think about all these men, women, and children who have left the heart of Dolpo to go to the low-lying valleys of grain.

The trail suddenly leaves the stream and climbs the mountain abruptly on our right. "It is too cold at the bottom of the gorges," grumbles Tilen, "and there are no pastures for the animals."

We catch up with Renzing Dorje. He still has his *yerka*, the ball of butter his wife applied to his forehead before his departure, to protect him on the road. When we departed, she had lifted the palm of her right hand toward the sky in a gesture of offering and also placed the yerka on my forehead, saying: *"Kale pe ha!*—Go slowly!" Then she had watched the caravan leave, absorbed in a silent prayer. The days preceding the great departure are busy for the lamas of Dolpo. From sunrise, they pass from house to house to call down the gods' blessings and to remove any obstacles or adversities.

The scent of juniper rises from the terraced roofs; the monks' ample dark red robes contrast with the sky. Lamps burn sheltered from the wind. Drum, conch, and bell: The ritual goes on, and the master of the house brings offerings of milk, yogurt, and chang to the

roof's four corners. "*Sooo! Sooo! Lha gyalo!*—May the gods be victorious!" Perched on the tips of prayer masts in the corners of the terrace, jackdaws wait their turn to share the scraps. It is time to leave the homeland for the grain route. "May the gods guide the caravanners' steps during these long months, and watch over the families who have stayed at home!"

Prayer flags are sewn into the long hair along the yaks' spines. Some yaks even have their horns colored with the red earth from Shey Gompa. They pant on the winding trail. A sling's dry smacking noise, the packsaddle squeaking, and hooves hammering the soft bed of chalk break the silence and echo on gorge walls swept by the wind. The caravanners' long modulated whistling encourages the animals in their efforts. Few words are exchanged until the evening camp. At the end of the afternoon, we reach a large shoulder at a good altitude.

"Hey, you over there! Ralden, listen to me! This is where we will stop tonight!" chants Tilen, in a deep and appeasing voice to his yak, a chant every caravanner improvises to calm his yaks.

"You with the white forehead! Come back!"

The yak-hair ropes are rapidly untied and the loads of salt fall heavily onto the ground. The packsaddles are taken off, and the animals move away. It is cold. I help the caravanners build a

(pages 146-47) Before the caravans depart, the yaks carry juniper bushes and sacks of dried dung, which will be used as fuel by those who will spend the winter in Saldang.

*A caravanner in
a storm.*

horseshoe-shaped shelter with heaps of salt sacks. I had anticipated tonight's stop when I saw the men amass some bushes and dried dung along the road to light the campfire. Before sunset, we will search for more sources to feed the fire, while the women will break the nearest stream's ice to make tea.

Soon the fires rise in the center of the six camps. The smoke burns our eyes, fills the atmosphere with its pungent smell, and makes our food taste very strange. We warm up around the flames, our frozen backs offered to the darkness. The ponies, dogs, and some goats are brought back and tied up, safe from wolves and leopards. The yaks can defend themselves and graze freely all night.

I drink countless cups of burning tea, my hands gripped tightly around the cup's hot wood. A heavy yak leg is making the rounds. The dagger blade shining in the flame's light cuts raw frozen slices of meat, which are sprinkled with salt and red pepper. The meat is tender and soft, and if some pieces of ice didn't crunch between my teeth, I would think I was eating a delicious sushi. Unless, of course, I have lost my ability to taste here, so high, so far, so tired and hungry.

An icy wind sweeps through the camp and seeps into the layers of my clothes. At 7 p.m., the thermometer I had left on the salt sacks indicates almost 14°F. "Tibetans never wash because it is so cold," Tilen had told me. "The dirt and fat form a naturally protective layer. Furthermore, it makes you less vulnerable to flea bites."

Seeing me knead the tsampa and butter in the tea with my hands, Tilen says, mischievously: "Don't you think that the *pak* tastes better when it is mixed with dirty hands?"

pak: a mixture of grilled barley flour and tea

I look around me. Like them, my wrinkles must be underlined with black lines, my hair must be shaggy and dirty. And my only pants resemble jeans only vaguely. Seeing a drop of hot tea freeze instantly when it touches my jacket, I challenge anybody to wash here. Basically, I love this life, this contact with nature. I like being dirty. I am happy, even flattered to share the intimacy of these uncouth

Tilen and his Tibetan pony.

people, to relax with them in the sumptuous Himalayan night.

The felt carpet and blankets that protect the yaks' spines from the heavy packsaddles serve as mattresses and blankets. The road dust, animal sweat, and heavy smell mix with the sweat and smell of the caravanners and the smell of the fire and form a strange odor that emanates from every being here.

Tilen slides a small sack of tsampa under my head as a cushion. I bury myself completely in my sleeping bag.

"You look like a caterpillar," he says, and bursts out laughing.

In the early morning Lhundrup and Chewong leave to look for the yaks. Tilen is already taking care of the fire, although he just woke up. He takes some hemp and a flint from his leather pocket and strikes a light. A small cloud of smoke appears. He blows softly to kindle his tiny fire. He delicately places the hemp between two small, well-dried pieces of yak dung while continuing to blow. A small, shy flame rises, and he places it religiously in the fireplace's center. He then piles yak dung all around it. Finally, he gets some blankets and fans the fire while sitting cross-legged. Thick, pungent smoke rises.

Still under her blankets, a woman places a pot filled with ice on the fire's three stones for tea. A three-year-old child awakens, searches for a breast, then, satisfied, plays with silver jewelry.

The yaks are driven by young men into the camp with the first rays of the sun. We eat quickly, then the women fold the sleeping bags and put away the utensils while the men go to the yaks. Calming the animals with their deep and soft voices, they bind the two rear feet together. Surprised, some animals jump away, spreading panic.

I too learn the work of the caravanners. I approach a yak slowly while clicking my tongue to let the animal know that I am coming. I

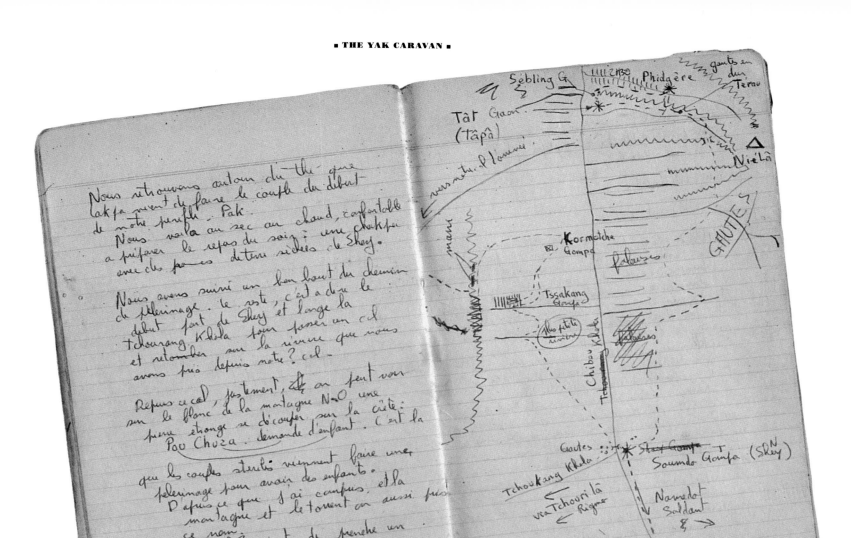

get to my knees and with my body alert, place the rope just above its hooves before tying the loop as Tilen taught me. The animal is peaceful. I risk scratching its shoulder, and its massive head turns around slowly. I feel the heat of its breath on my cheek.

Once the yaks are fitted with their packsaddles and loaded with their hundred pounds of salt, they are untied.

"*Touuuuuu kee yoo!*" The caravanners' shouts break the silence. The caravan is set slowly into motion.

We reach Kimba La just before midday. It is the summit of the first pass. We see the gigantic barrier separating us from the lower valleys. The mountains shine, covered by icy snow. I suddenly feel my smallness and fragility.

Two thousand yaks and hundreds of people in small groups will soon use the trail. The trail continues as far as the eye can see. We stop every two or three days for a day to let the yaks graze and rest. We should reach the *Rong-pa* in three weeks if all goes well. We leave the mountains' jagged crests and descend a slope of dark scree. The men joyously descend, as if to free themselves from the painful climb.

Rong-pa: People of the valleys

After crossing Nyelde's large rocky plain, we begin to climb the Lagmo Shey Pass. Just before we reach the snow, Tilen decides to camp in a small sheltered basin covered with dry and silky grass. He sits down and uses both hands to tear the golden carpet covering the ground to fill his felt boots for the approaching cold. At night around the fire, the men clean their faces with a bit of tea. I hold my hands to the fire. Tilen places one hand on mine. "How it is big, how it is cold," he says, taking my hand into his calloused palms to warm it.

"You know, before coming to Dolpo, Diane had never seen snow," I told him. "There are no mountains in her country, which is surrounded by a gigantic ocean."

I told him about coral, the tree that grows under the ocean. I told him about the men who eat fish and use boats as transportation. "You have traveled so much and seen so many things," he tells me. "Why do you come here so often, to work and freeze with us while you have a house and a family waiting for you in Kathmandu?"

I told him that even as a child I had dreamed about these mountains and caravans.

"Other foreigners have also told me they liked Dolpo. But why did they not stay? Why did they not build their houses here? Why did they not raise their children here?" Tilen asks.

It is cold this night. The edges of my sleeping bag, which I had pulled tightly around my face, are frozen. Lhundrup and Karma get up and dress quickly. They leave to look for the yaks, tiny silhouettes in the vastness of the mountains. A kind of torpor holds the landscape until the sun's rays finally light the summits and descend toward us. To warm up, I stomp my feet on the frozen ground and go from one camp to the next. These few moments before the sun rises are the coldest of the day.

Sitting around the fire, a lama wrapped in his thick lokpa recites the prayer of Drolma, the travelers' protective divinity. His body

The yak caravans, loaded with salt, cross a pass in the Himalaya leading to the land of grain.

The caravanners serve tea in the circle of salt sacks protecting them from the icy wind. A frozen yak leg is on the left. On the right lies ice to be melted.

rocks back and forth to the rhythm of a chant the other yak-pas have joined in. They regularly throw their butter and tsampa offerings into the fire so that the road may be favorable. The power of the gods and demons constantly surfaces here. Gestures, events, and daily actions all find a purpose in the spiritual world. Their interpretation is a true science, whose ultimate goal is to favor the positive or combat the negative effects. Ceremonies, prayers, exorcisms, divinations, and offerings—I used to smile about these things. But I have learned to respect what I used to term superstition or naiveté. These beliefs have enabled these people to survive in one of the most inhospitable places on earth for almost 2,000 years. If I were alone here, how long would I survive?

The herd reaches the camp two hours later. Left to roam freely at night, the yaks sometimes venture far to graze. The yak-pa always are careful to camp between the yaks and their village, because the animals have a tendency to return to the village the first few days. At the summit of the Lagmo Shey Pass, the yak-pa tighten the harnesses for the descent.

That evening, we stop on a crest where we see the small blue triangle of Tso at the end of the gorges. The lower-lying cliffs are inhabited by snow leopards, and the animals will be sent up a stream. During my first trip with the caravans several years ago, a young yak was killed here by a big cat.

The sun shines and the pastures are abundant. Tilen decides to grant us all a day's rest. The men sit in the sun, protected from the wind by salt-sack walls. Some of them mend a boot, repair a packsaddle or a rope, or play the lute. The younger ones climb into the high pastures to see if all is well.

The next day, we follow a trail cut into a mountainside until we reach the base of the third pass, Baga La, where a Karang caravan is already camped. The following day it leaves at dawn, and we observe the yaks' slow progression on the winding trails above us.

The yaks cross Nyelde, the section of trail just before the first pass on leaving Dolpo.

Tilen decides to rest a day here before attacking the pass. During these days of rest I really notice the slowness of time and the caravan's frailness in this grandiose and pitiless universe. Several years ago, a storm took a caravan by surprise between these two passes, which are located at an altitude of 16,000 feet. Sixty yaks died in the snow, and the caravanners survived by a miracle. After having exhausted their meager provisions of tsampa and tea, they ended up eating the leather soles of their *seumbas*, Tibetan boots.

The sky is dark blue now and cloudless. The temperature drops abruptly during the night, but the night is extraordinarily clear. The glaciers are fluorescent. In the morning, the dogs that had slept coiled up are covered with frost.

The next day, after having crossed Baga La, we camp in the Ringmo Valley near a small forest, the first one for many months.

I had stayed so long in Dolpo, in the region of arid landscapes, that I had forgotten about the diversity of pleasures offered by nature. Once again I could chew on a succulent grass blade, smell the earth's perfume, listen to the song of birds and the wind whispering, remembering the colors and varieties of shadows in forest vegetation.

I no longer feel the dry land and uneven stones under my feet, but a carpet of tender moss crackling with dead leaves. I even delight in recognizing insect noises. Even the light is different, less contrasted and harsh than up where everything is black or white.

I am not the only one today to feel this sudden joy.

A child feels the bark of an old pine tree and has fun with a resin drop. Sitting on the trail, fathers teach their children how to break hard nutshells and extract the meat with a needle. I see the marveling eyes, the small mouths half open, astonished. Those who had never before crossed the mountain barrier that isolates the Hidden Land discover a new world today. Of course they had heard about it. But how can you imagine what a forest is when you are born in a world without forests? How can you imagine this luxury when your only known home is in a mountain desert? Several days later, we leave Ringmo's wooded valley and enter once again into an austere canyon. Tilen is worried. While the highest of the four passes still separates us from the Rong-pa land, the November sky is veiled by a thick cloud cover. This night, we pitch the cotton tent for the first time. It covers

Three tiny caravans climb toward the Baga La (17,400 feet).

the circle of sacks. Little is said around the fire. All are preoccupied with the weather. The evening wind is less cold than usual.

Tilen silently observes the starless night. Then he takes some salt crystals out of a woolen sack, rolls them in his hand, and places them solemnly in the fire. Anxious eyes converge on the flames. The crystals burst with the heat. All faces relax. The salt is dry and the storm will not come until tomorrow. "If the salt is humid," explains Tilen, "it does not burst. That is a sign of bad weather."

In the middle of the night, a deep rumble suddenly awakens me. The earth vibrates. The dogs bark. There is total darkness. I instinctively curl up against the salt sacks. The rumbling becomes more distant, then a second tremor shakes the ground. My companions are also awake. I hear bits of smothered sentences, the murmur of prayers. Calm and the silence of the night return.

I regain my breath. A nervous laugh begins at the other end of the tent. Tilen coughs. I find my lamp. Earthquakes often shake the Himalayan chain and push it each time a bit closer to the sky.

At the summit of Kagmara La, the men deposit a stone on the cairn as a sign of grace, then move on. Our hearts are lighter. The caravan has crossed the last pass and is descending into the land of grain.

That night, Lhundrup plays his dramien. Joy and relief animate the voices. The dancers circle the fire with their arms interlaced and jewelry shining in the firelight. Lhundrup improvises a song about the improvident Wangyal, who was too lazy to mend his boots and lost his soles in a storm. His toes had turned black when he reached the village. Those who had escaped freezing this time laughed.

The next day, the yaks are grouped on the bank of a stream that goes down the glaciers. The *lamba*, the lead yak whose head is decorated with a red yak tail, is hesitant to go forward. Its mountain universe is rooted in winter, very different from the moving and gurgling element that it suddenly must brave. The caravanners encourage it, the best of yaks, the one that will lead the others.

Tired of waiting, one of the men picks up a stone from the path and puts it in his yak-hair slingshot. He hesitates, gets a good hold, looks for a good angle. His legs anchored, he whirls slowly. Suddenly, the sling opens, relaxes, and the stone is hurled toward its target. It hits a yak's rump. A wave sweeps through the herd to the head animal, which finally enters the stream's tumultuous waters.

In spite of the cold, some animals stop in the middle to drink, their long fur floating in the current. Men and women are gripping their loads and cross on the animals' backs. The dogs are left behind. They roam for a long time on the other bank, howling with chagrin and fright before braving the torrent. Tonight, the dogs timidly crouch next to the fire, their frozen coats resembling strange carapaces.

(pages 162-63)
Tilen and his yaks en route to the land of grain.

*Eight-year-old
Pemal Angyal
crosses Kimbu La.
Before him to the
south rises the
mountain barrier
he must cross to
reach the land of
grain.*

*(pages 166-67)
The caravan climbs
Kimbu La (17,400
feet). Behind and to
the north, the
mountains mark the
Chinese border.*

The yaks sometimes use a trail running near the lake at Ringmo.

(pages 170-71) Finally, the caravans enter the deep forests covering the slopes of the southern Himalaya.

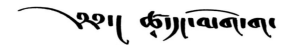

Salt and Grain

We reach the first villages three days later in the Rimi Valley, the land of grain. The caravans disperse. Some stay in Hurikot; others will go on to Tapa Gaon. Every family in Dolpo knows an ista in the lower valleys, a privileged partner with whom they negotiate the exchange. But the close ties between the Dolpo-pa and Rong-pa have deteriorated. Since the invasion of Tibet and the closing of the borders, the Chinese have so extensively rationed the quantity of salt allocated to the Dolpo-pa that it is now insufficient to provide for the needs of the inhabitants of the south. They are therefore forced to purchase salt coming from the Indian Ocean. This salt is less expensive than the salt from Tibet, because the roads coming from India have come closer and closer to the Himalayan heart.

The Rong-pa prefer the salt of the north, which is famous for its energetic properties. It reinforces the immunity of their animals, while the Indian salt causes itching and weakens the animals' resistance to sicknesses.

Women husking grain on Chuma's terraced roofs.

࿓༎ སྟོད་ལ་པོ་པ་ཆུ་ཁྱེར་རས་ཐབ་མ་གཏགས་མཆུ་ལ་སྐྱེལ་རེད་

ༀ༅། རི་མོ་འདི་ཅུང་ སྐྱེ་འཇིན་ ནོར་ཕྱུགས་ ཡིན་བཀུར་ཤིས་ཕོག།

While Tilen watches, a Rong-pa fills one of Lhundrup's sacks with the corn that was just exchanged for salt.

In spite of this, the exchange rate of Tibetan salt lessens in Rimi.

We drink many cups of rakshi after the customary words, sitting around a fireplace in the two rooms reserved for winter visitors. It is the encounter of two worlds, Tibet and India, the encounter of two cultures and two religions. News is exchanged in Nepali, the common language. "This year, the Chinese once again lowered the salt quotas." One inquires about the death of a daughter-in-law, the snow on the passes, the state of the livestock. Budhi Dhami, the ista, wears a turban and is dressed in cotton. He complains of the poor monsoon and the meager corn harvest. Curious villagers enter and sit close to the fire. They counted Tilen's salt sacks when they passed them on the terrace. The *chillum* passes from hand to hand, and the local tobacco's thick smoke is eagerly inhaled. The rakshi begins to take

chillum: a clay pipe

effect. Outside, the children break nuts between two stones. It is already late when Tilen finally gets to the heart of the matter. He says he would exchange a measure of salt for four measures of corn. A heavy silence ensues. All turn to the ista, the village chief. He says that is impossible. He can only offer two measures of corn for one measure of salt.

Last year, the Dolpo-pa had obtained three measures, and four measures two years ago. Tilen refuses to exchange under four.

"This is about the survival of my people," he argues.

"If we do not reach an agreement, we will not let your yaks graze here during the winter," the village chief replies firmly.

A disapproving murmur rises among the Dolpo-pa. They do not change their minds this night, but it is decided that both parties will have three days to agree on the exchange rate.

Tilen is solemn. As usual, those who accompanied him trust his experience. As long as he has not reached a decision, no agreement will be concluded in the valley. Rumors are circulating. It is said that in the western valley of Tichurong, the rate is three for one. Others say that it is only two for one. Tilen threatens to exchange the salt

A Rong-pa woman threshes grain.

(pages 178-79) Talphi's main road. The buildings are built like staircases on the hillside. The ladder beams enable the villagers to go from one house to the next.

elsewhere if he does not receive at least three and a half measures of grain for one measure of salt. The Rong-pa reply that they would not only forbid the Dolpo-pa's yaks to graze, but that they would also add a tax of five rupees per person and per yak passing through their lands. The discussions are unending. Spirits are bathed with alcohol, but Tilen remains calm, dignified, and in charge. I watch him surreptitiously empty his cup of rakshi on the clay floor behind him.

The third day, after much negotiation, the two chiefs agree on two and a half measures of corn for one measure of salt. The Dolpo-pa are bitter. They have never had to accept such a low offer. But do they really have a choice? At least their yaks are allowed to graze. Three days later, we drive the yaks to the fresh grass.

Another caravan joins us above the villages. I curiously touch the fadse and feel large rough salt crystals. Tilen smiles:

"I hid the salt in the mountains. If you show too much salt, the rate will get even lower. The exchange we just did will only help us subsist. We must go farther and exchange the remaining salt in Chaudhabise. It is said that the men there are hungry for salt."

Once again, Tilen has shown himself worthy of his peers' confidence. He knew how to appease the villagers from Rimi, assure the grazing rights for his yaks, and avoid the pass-through tax, while still keeping the possibility of exchanging a third of the salt for a doubtless better rate than we had gotten here.

The women and children stay in the villages, and the journey continues for the men and yaks.

We enter into a vast forest above a small pass. We are at nearly 10,000 feet. Yaks are more fragile and sensitive to sicknesses at this altitude. Tilen scrutinizes the water before allowing his animals to drink. Some yaks had died on their way home to Dolpo two years ago. People say their brains were destroyed by leeches that they had swallowed while drinking water from the lower valleys.

Four days later, the large fertile valley of Chaudhabise opens before us. We notice the abundance of water, the forests' grandeur, and the richness of the black earth. Tilen decides to go to the last village, Chuma, whose chief is known to the Dolpo-pa. Word of mouth has preceded us, and they are waiting for us. Soon after the tent is pitched, a large-scale discussion ensues around the fire. But this night we do not talk about salt or grain. I smile when I notice the apparent disinterest that they force themselves to show. A distaff

(pages 182-83) Until 1986, sheep caravans from Jumla and Chaudhabise still climbed to Dolpo to look for salt.

Nanda Lal and his nephew shear sheep on the terrace of their house.

dances in Chime Renzing's hands. Nanda Lal Thapa, the village chief, reminisces about Dolpo, which he has often visited. The curious Rong-pa gather at the tent's entrance. They comment on the situation with hushed voices while knitting.

"It has been a long time since the yaks have come here!"

The next morning, after Nanda Lal has brought an armful of apples, the exchange rate is finally discussed. Like Tilen, Nanda Lal is the village chief, and he must defend his villagers' interests. When Tilen asks for five measures of grain for one measure of salt, Nanda Lal smiles and offers three. Tilen sits in the back of his tent, his tea cup placed on a stone in front of him. He turns toward the group of spectators that has formed. Once again the tone rises.

"We have brought the salt to the threshold of your houses, and you do not offer us more than in Hurikot? Those of you who know Dolpo know of the trials we had to endure to get to this magnificent valley, where you have everything in abundance: water, wood, wheat, buckwheat, and even corn."

His voice is strong and clear. After every sentence he pauses, as if to give his audience time to assimilate and understand his well-reasoned arguments. "But what would all this taste like without salt? Salt, as you well know, is much more precious than the gold you give your women."

The Rong-pa remain immobile and silent. The distaffs no longer move. A chillum even goes out in a shepherd's hand. The dignity and survival of these men is decided in only a few sentences.

I also am touched. I also wait. What could one add after such a discourse? Who would have the audacity to contradict Tilen, the chief of Saldang's caravan? Finally, the rate is fixed at four measures of corn for one measure of salt. But Tilen, who decidedly is having a great day, does not want to leave things there.

"You could offer some food to us during the exchange. We came to

Nanda Lal Thapa and his pipe.

your village, the farthest one in the valley." Nanda Lal offers a *mana*—about a pint—of corn for every bag of salt.

"What! That is not even the mice's share!"

Tilen gets five manas of corn per bag of salt.

It took three days for the exchange. Hands exchanged salt and grain on the terraces. After the transaction, the men from Dolpo took back a pinch of salt that they had just exchanged, so they would not lose their good luck. This good luck helped them once again cross the mountains without problems, and it helped their intelligent chief exchange the Tibetan salt at an acceptable rate. The golden corn is loaded into the bags that were used to transport the salt. Then the caravanners use the long needles that they always carry in their chubas to sew up the openings. Tilen caresses a full bag with his large calloused hand:

"It looks like a well-filled stomach!" he says with a satisfied smile.

*Red beans brought
from the village are
exchanged for salt
from India.*

THE RONG-PA VILLAGES

During the days of exchange I explored the life of the valley people. Their villages have narrow, tortuous, smelly streets. The ground is uneven and strewn with mud, straw, stones, and excrement, into which small family dogs stick their noses.

The people are surprised and curious when they see me. They timidly approach and begin a conversation. It is difficult for me to understand them. The Nepali of the west is different from that of Kathmandu, but I can still reply. They, on the other hand, do not understand me. They decide that the foreigner—the America, as they call me—does not speak their language. They go away disappointed, shrugging their shoulders, and wondering about this foreigner who came so far to see their village but with whom they cannot even communicate. Frustrated, I catch up with them. I insist that they *can* understand the words coming out of my mouth. But no, how could they understand a foreign language? Finally, I grab a man's shoulder and slowly separate each word: *"Ma nepali bolchou! Ale pharak tcha holla tara nepali ho!*—I speak Nepali! Perhaps a bit differently than you, but it is Nepali!"

A face lights up and laughter spreads.

"Hoooh! Nepali boltcha!—Oh! He speaks Nepali!"

And they invite me into their houses and proudly show me their children.

THE HOUSE OF THE GODS

Nanda Lal Thapa, the village chief, belongs to the Chetri caste, the second one after the Brahmans, the Hindu priests. He leads me into the village one evening and through a low door. The room is lit with a

A young Rong-pa shepherd carries salt to his sheep.

few oil lamps. Red and white fabric strips hang from the ceiling beams. A wall in the back is decorated with primitive wooden statues. A dozen villagers are already sitting down. Their faces are very different from the Tibetan faces with which I just traveled. The Rong-pa have less angular, rounder and darker faces. I sit next to an old man who holds his granddaughter on his knees. A swing-plow with a wooden plowshare hangs on the wall. A chicken broods in a corner. The clay floor was covered this morning with a layer of purifying cow dung.

Nanda Lal sits facing me against a board wall where a face shows through a tiny opening. Two men dressed in white sit next to my companion. One of them rings a bell. The other wears a long braid wound in a spiral around the top of his head. He is immobile and sits cross-legged with his head lowered. He is the Dhami, the village shaman. I soon learn that he is Nanda Lal's son.

Other visitors come and sit close together in the house of gods, as the grandfather on my left had defined it. He suddenly elbows me and points with his chin in the direction of the man with the braid. The man with the braid yawns and lets his head roll slowly on his shoulders. His eyes are closed. His face is contorted with uncontrollable grimaces, which he is apparently trying to mask with his hands. The bell rings regularly, irritatingly. Everyone looks at the man. His torso begins to heave, and his braid has fallen down to his belt. Copper, gold, and silver rings shine on his hands. Suddenly the Dhami takes the bell from his assistant and goes to sit down cross-legged among the wooden gods in the back of the temple. A square of fabric holding a pile of uncooked rice is placed in front of him. His hand flattens the grain pyramid. A strapping man steps out of the

crowd of spectators and sits next to the shaman, who is now possessed by the god. He salutes him by inclining his head, his hands joined in front of his forehead. The man's hatchet was stolen in the forest.

Kal Das, Nanda Lal's son, the shaman from Chuma, reads the future in the grain lying in front of him.

The shaman sweeps through the grain with his hand, draws strange arabesques, deposits a pinch on his palm, carefully reads the omen, and says: "Your hatchet was not stolen. You could not find the place where you had left it. Sleep with the pinch of grain under your pillow. In your dream you will see the place you have forgotten."

My neighbor has awakened his granddaughter and brings her before the oracle. Pus runs out of the child's ear. The Dhami leans over her, whispers a mantra, and softly blows on her face.

Another man worries if next Tuesday will be a favorable day for the caravan's departure to the south. The diviner takes a handful of grain, which he slowly pours onto his palm.

His eyes fix on the silky stream. "No," he says dryly.

"But! All has been arranged with the other caravanners. We must leave together. We could make an offering, a sacrifice!" the shepherd protests, suddenly very nervous.

"It is not that easy...but tell me...weren't you supposed to bring back a bell for the temple last year?" the Dhami asks.

"I was sick. I will bring it next time!" the shepherd replies.

The diviner becomes impatient and, without listening to the answer, whispers a prayer, throws a few pinches of rice into the audience, and starts with the next case.

It is late when the villagers get up to leave. The caravanner returns to see the shaman and beg him for help.

The shaman responds, "*La. Thik cha!*—That is good, that is good. Take this rice and put a bit on your door lintel on Tuesday. Distribute the rest on your herd. And then sacrifice a lamb on the altar of the gods in Ranga Chautara! But do not forget the bell!"

This is how I learned that Nanda Lal and the last herds of the valley would soon head south to search for the indispensable salt.

Nanda Lal grinds grain in his water mill.

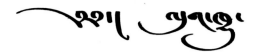

The Sheep Caravans

Nanda Lal walks slowly on his bowed legs. He carries a goatskin and a loom on his back wrapped in tent material. He uses the goatskin as a mattress and unfolds the loom every afternoon at the camp. Goats and sheep rub against his thick, brown, wool pants. Without stopping, he extracts a baked clay chillum from the folds of his large cotton belt, which he has wrapped several times around his waist. He fills the chillum with tobacco from his waistcoat. He extracts a pad of steel, a flint, and some hemp from a small wool bag. Nanda Lal looks into the distance. The trail climbs through a pine forest. The woolly flux of animals slowly advances. The animals are walking close together. Turning against the breeze, the shepherd lights his chillum again. Soon a tiny cloud of smoke rises. He then delicately lays down the fire, which smolders on the pipe's tobacco, and brings the pipe to his lips. He inhales slowly with his eyes closed. Nanda Lal keeps the smoke in his lungs for a long time, then ejects it with a very satisfied breath. The chillum then passes from one

Nanda Lal Thapa among his sheep.

shepherd to the next before finally being put back into the belt.

Every man carries a chillum in the west of Nepal, and every house has its own tobacco field. The pipe of baked clay is such an integral part of this region that walking distances are measured in chillums: "From here to there, it takes about…uhmmm…three chillums."

The trail narrows and the bags carried by the goats and sheep catch on the bushes. The day ends every evening at camp with the distribution of sacks filled with red beans, which are cultivated in Chaudhabise.

"Oh Vaida! Oh Vaida!—Stop! Stop!" shouts Nanda Lal, as he pushes his way through the herd to rescue a goat about to strangle itself with its load, which has slid to the ground.

Nanda Lal picks up the sack, and the goat tries to escape. He catches the goat by its coat and immobilizes it with one quick gesture, sticking the goat's head between his legs. He loads her again and carefully tightens the rope passing under the animal's tail. The Chang Tang nomads have always used goats and sheep as pack animals. Nanda Lal has his own version of the story concerning the origin of this practice.

"Before, our ancestors did not know anything about trade. They lived off the fruit of their land and their goat and sheep herds, which gave them wool, milk, meat, and leather.

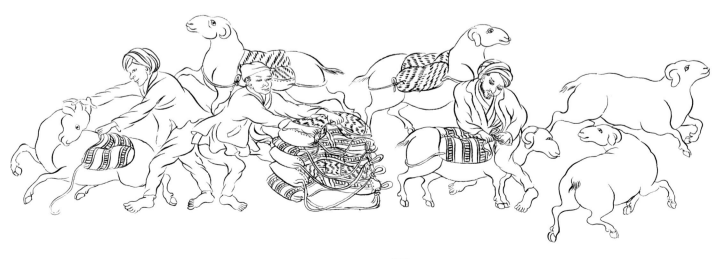

"One day, a young boy got lost in the forest. Night had already fallen when he saw a fire at the foot of a tree. An old man with a turban was cooking peacefully. A large pile of sacks lay next to him. He politely asked the newcomer to share his meal and offered him a blanket. It was still night when the young boy woke up, but the old man had rekindled the fire. The young man saw all the forest animals in the moving light of the flames. There were deer, wolves, leopards, and bears patiently waiting to be loaded. The man with the turban asked his young companion to accompany him and to help him with his work. They went into the deepest part of the forest, climbed mountains, and visited villages the child had never heard of. They ate delicious and unknown food. The old man's work consisted of transporting and exchanging the food, aided by wild animals. The child was finally found by his father many days later, near the spring where he had disappeared. The young boy described his adventure to his father and told him about Balkuna, the teachings of the forest god. This is how," concludes Nanda Lal, "our ancestors, who were farmers and shepherds, also became merchants."

(pages 198-99) Nanda Lal's sheep, loaded with red beans, leave for the south following the exchange of Tibetan salt for grain.

Caravans pass
through Dailekh.
The shepherd's long
bamboo poles
control the herd.

(pages 202-03)
Curious villagers
are sheltered from
the rain while
watching the
caravans pass.

A baby sleeps at the bottom of a doko, the head swaying to the rhythm of the mother's steps. The dogs happily roam about, freely running from left to right. Their bells ring. They wear chains around their necks. Since the caravan has entered the forests that cover the sides of the pass through Chakhure Lekh, Nanda Lal has placed large spiked, metallic collars around the necks of the animals to defend them from the possible attack of a leopard.

Nanda Lal wears a brown wool hank around his left wrist, which he spins while walking. The distaff circles at his fingertips and comes down as the thread extends. He brings it up before it touches the ground and winds the thread around the wool ball.

It is 11 o'clock. The animals have walked for six hours, and some of them begin to lie down along the road and only get up when a shepherd approaches. The stifling heat affects the sheep and goats. This is why we start before daybreak. Furthermore, the Rong-pa shepherds cannot let their animals graze at night freely like the Dolpo-pa do with their yaks. Goats and sheep are too often the target of predators. They therefore must graze in the afternoon under the eye of shepherds. They then return at the end of the day to the camp and spend the night guarded by dogs.

Nanda Lal decides to stop tonight at the foot of the last long climb leading to Chakhure Lekh. The animal line grows, a large moving spot in the midst of the clearing. We pile the *loukals* onto a bed of stones to keep them away from the wet ground. The youngsters fetch water and wood. Nanda Lal pitches the tent. The women prepare the *chapatis* with corn flour and cook a red bean soup.

loukal:
a double bag of
wool and leather

chapati:
pancake made with
wheat and corn

Thousands of animals from Jumla, Chaudhabise, and Rimi use this trail at this time of year. The camps are occupied almost every day in

this migratory season. The fire cinders do not even have time to cool down before new caravanners revive them.

Two main routes lead to the southern trails from this region. The route we follow passes through Chakhure Lekh, Barakot, and Jajankot as far as Bhotechaur. The other route is located more to the west. It is called the Raja Marga, the royal pathway, because it crosses through Sinja and Dullu, the ancient capitals of the Malla kingdom, which became wealthy from the trade between Tibet and India from the 12th to the 14th centuries. When the snow falls too early in Chakhure Lekh, Nanda Lal uses that route. It is longer but its passes are more accessible.

After the meal, Nanda Lal unfolds his loom between two pegs and the large belt he wears. He weaves the thread he made during the

A caravanner relaxes near the fire, while lighting a chillum. The shepherds often sleep next to their animals in the forest to protect them from wolves and leopards.

walk. The travelers descending from the pass stop to smoke a chillum and exchange some news: "Yes, there is snow at the summit of the pass, but the trail is clear. The sheep did not sink in when we crossed early this morning. A horse died yesterday after it broke a leg. The vultures are having a feast."

The sun disappears quickly behind the crests, and our camp becomes cold. Nanda Lal, who has fallen asleep, suddenly awakens and goes to meet the animals that have returned to the camp. He stays alone in the midst of the herd and distributes pats and quieting words. The other shepherds look at him with respect.

Yesterday, I asked Nanda Lal if he preferred his life in the village or his life on the road. He smiled, shrugged his shoulders and, with a gesture of his head, pointed to his sheep. The animals are more than just a means of survival; they also mean adventure and travel for their masters. Life on the road is harsh, but they prefer it to life in the villages. The people are nomads at heart.

Later on, when I compared the Dolpo people to those of the valleys, Nanda Lal added: "People do not resemble each other. Their skin color, language, way of life, and gods are often different. But deep down inside, don't we have the same bones?"

From crest to crest, villages to pastures, we took three months to reach Bhotechaur, the far end of the route from India. Pickaxes and miner's bars help the road penetrate deeper into the Himalaya every day. There, the red beans brought back from the village will be exchanged for Indian salt. The sale of a few sheep and of blankets woven en route will allow the travelers to obtain paper money.

A young shepherd returns the sheep to the camp for the night after having watched the animals in the pastures.

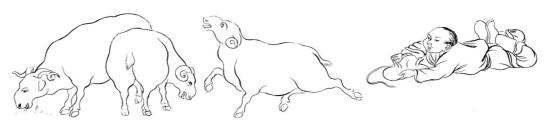

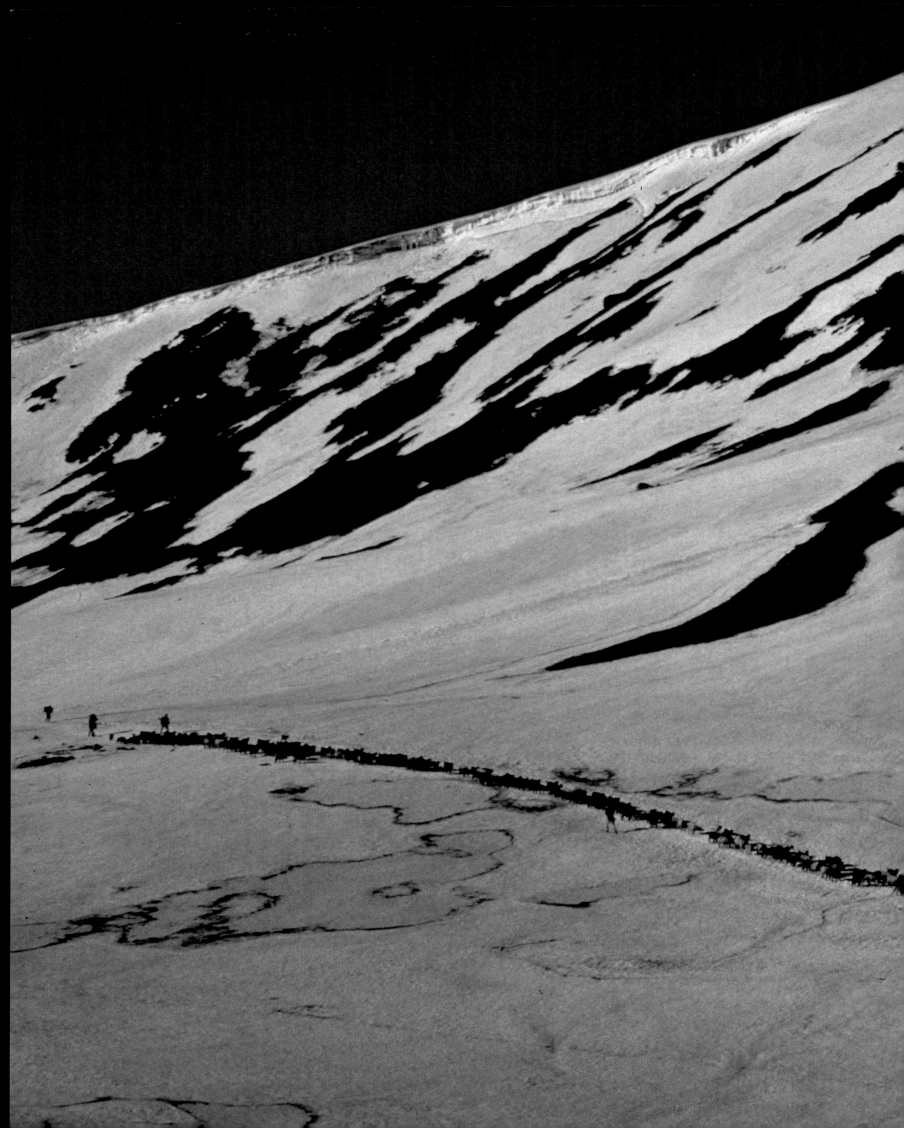

*After three months
on the trail, the
caravans arrive at
the road from India
that leads deeper
into the mountains
every day.*

*(pages 208-09)
Nanda Lal spins
thread at the camp
while Rupa Karki,
his daughter-in-
law, cooks corn
pancakes.*

*(pages 210-11)
Rupa Karki and
her daughter in
the camp.*

*(pages 212-13)
A caravan crosses
snow from the
previous year,
which covers the
pass through
Chakhure Lekh
(14,000 feet).*

*(following pages)
In March the
caravans leave the
fertile southern hills
and bring back
Indian salt to their
villages in the
foothillls of the
Himalaya.*

प्रधान्नी

Pradhani

The caravans loaded with salt begin their long climb to the north in February. Tonight's camp is located on a large overhang protected by two gigantic, sacred trees, which watch over the ruins of a small Hindu temple.

In the morning, Nanda Lal comes down the winding trail leading to the village of Daulakot. The white, thatched-roof houses spread over a complex chessboard of terraced fields. Some are still covered with golden barley or wheat punctuated by the moving dots of harvesters. Others are already harvested and show the gray earth and straw eaten by the village goats and sheep. Some already plowed fields show the fertile land's red ocher bowels. Buffalo roam under the wooden balconies. Chickens fly away at our approach. Dogs bark ferociously.

Nanda Lal stops by every house to say hello, gives some news, and asks if there is any grain to buy or exchange for the salt carried by his sheep. He starts the conversation and extracts a few mono-syllables from the obviously embarrassed inhabitants. Without

A Chetri grandmother and her grandson.

exception they answer no, with their eyes fixed to the ground. A pair of oxen tied to a pole in the center of the threshing area turn incessantly, knee-deep in straw, their hooves separating the grain from the chaff.

Since we reached the valley at the southern foot of Chakhure Lekh, rumors have circulated about a generous harvest. This is why Nanda Lal does not seem worried, in spite of being tired from the road, the frosty welcome, discouraging responses, and frowning faces. He apparently understands the rules of a game that I as yet do not. He walks slowly, his hands crossed behind his back, peacefully contemplating the village life, until he reaches the entrance of a long house with a slate roof.

A man carries a gigantic sheaf of wheat, under which he disappears. He lets his load fall in the paved courtyard. He wipes his sweaty forehead and goes into the house. Two children come out laughing, pancakes held under their arms. Another one goes into the house carrying three dark, wooden receptacles from which a stream of milk overflows through an unlikely cover of dead leaves. The sewing machine of a traveling tailor hums in the balcony's shadow.

A young Rong-pa shepherdess carries all her belongings and a rooster in a bamboo basket.

While waiting, we sit on a small wall. Nanda Lal picks up an ear of grain, crushes it between his palms, blows away the husk, and examines the grain.

The pass through Chakhure Lekh, the highest the sheep caravanners must cross to go south to Bhotechaur.

**badji:
a grandfather,
in Nepali**

"Oh! *Badji!* You are there! What do you give me for my barley? Salt or silver? Come on, climb," a silhouette leaning over the balcony says with authority. One can recognize the richness of a house by the number of copper and brass pots shining in the dim light of the main room. The *gangro* with the rounded stomach is used for water, the *kourkoulo* with the large opening is used to cook rice during festival days, the *ouno* holds grain and is sealed with a mixture of dung and clay, the small *bokuto* is used to cook lentils. In a corner, a young boy cleans the brass pots with a wet towel and ashes.

Muni Basnet must be as old as Nanda Lal, about 60 years. She

*(pages 222-23)
Rupa Kali leads the
sheep caravan on
the trail.*

Held securely in place by a rope, a child is carried in a doko.

invites us to sit down and serves us a bowl of rakshi. In spite of her frail body, her voice is high and impetuous. She is the mistress of the house and distributes tasks to her numerous nephews, sisters, grandsons, granddaughters, and other workers. But her authority carries well beyond her house. She is the Pradhani, the mistress of Daulakot, known and respected for her competence when it comes to transactions. Nobody in the village can take on the responsibility of trading until she herself has established the exchange rate.

Nanda Lal and the Pradhani have known each other for a long time. Until recently they exchanged the village grain for Tibetan salt, as was done for generations before them. But for half a dozen years the building of roads has brought paper money, which did not exist before, as well as cheaper Indian salt. The trade has changed. The money obtained from selling sheep and wool blankets is now used along with salt to buy grain.

They discuss the price while drinking small sips of rakshi in brass bowls. The grain is brought to Nanda Lal. He is the first one to recognize its quality. But....

pathi:
volume measure
equal to 8 manas,
thus 2 gallons

"Ten rupees for a *pathi*!"

After many cups of rakshi and long discussions, the Pradhani becomes impatient: "Will we speak this way until our heads hurt?"

"No," says Nanda Lal, "but we all must get our fair share."

The shepherd adds, comparing their negotiations to the encounter between a snarling dog and a passerby: "It is no more necessary to kill the dog than it is to break the stick. They are both useful. This year the harvest has given you more than enough. Will you let the insects and mice eat what you do not wish to sell?"

The two merchants finally agree on the same price as the last three years: eight rupees for a pathi, or a corresponding quantity in salt.

"Do you know," says the Pradhani with false exasperation, "that they all wish me dead in the village? They always pretend that I do not sell expensively enough!"

However, the dung that seals the jar covers is broken, the grain flows, and the Pradhani sends her people to thresh and sift some more barley.

The mistress of the house takes up her work and busies herself, much as the bees nesting in the house wall. We hear the stifled noise of a pounder from the outside. The barley crackles on the bamboo mats while the chaff flies away on the wind.

During the two days of threshing, exchanges, and sifting, the Pradhani's house is bathed in a golden halo. A kind of joyous fever has overtaken everybody. It is fun to touch the grain. The pathis fill up and empty in a silky stream. The barley flows between the fingers and expands into a large golden heap on the blankets of black goat hair. The shepherds sit cross-legged on goatskin blankets.

A young man uses a long stick to push the grain into the sacks, which swell and become round and hard like pancakes. The openings are sewn up and cow dung is applied to the spots where loose stitches have let the grain escape.

Nanda Lal descends to the village and lets the young caravanners take charge of the load.

A Rong-pa's light shoes were wrapped with sackcloth because of the cold during the crossing of Chakhure Lekh.

The rumor has spread:

"Eight rupees per pathi! Eight rupees per pathi!" But the villagers hide their enthusiasm when the shepherd arrives.

"No," they still answer, "but come in just the same and share a chillum!" The faces become more joyous and the tongues loosen in the house's soft light. Sacks are taken out from the dark corners. Nanda Lal weighs them.

Now that the price is fixed it is not necessary to speak about an exchange rate. The shepherd joins his hands on his chest after each transaction, bows slightly, and goes to the next house.

He goes to a villager who had asked him for three goats six months ago. The man had wanted to sacrifice the goats to the local gods. He had promised to pay in grain after the harvest.

After six days in Daulakot, money, salt, and grain have partially exchanged hands. On the morning of our departure the villagers offer pancakes, lentils, garlic, and red pepper for the journey. Nanda Lal puts his presents into the fabric of his turban, which he carries in a bundle.

"Pheri aunos!—See you next time!" shout the villagers.

The herd moves between the harvested fields.

"You see," says Nanda Lal, turning back to the village, "they are nice people. They only waited for the Pradhani's decision!"

In the beginning of May, five months after our departure, Nanda Lal and his caravans have returned to Chuma with the shipment of Indian salt and a bit of grain for their people.

The yaks are still in the pastures. It is springtime and the snow on the passes to Dolpo begins to melt. In the beginning of June, the yak caravans climb to their mountains loaded with grain. Thus the cycle of exchanges, the quest for salt, grain, and grass is perpetuated.

Yet someday the price of Tibetan salt will completely collapse, because of the new roads leading to the south. How will the Dolpo-pa survive then?

When the time has come to bid good-bye to Tilen, he reassures me: "We Tibetans, we will adapt once again. But when you return to Dolpo, bring something to sell. Why take on such hardship if it's not for business?" ☐

The Pradhani
measures the grain
that Nanda Lal has
exchanged.

A young shepherd returns the sheep to the camp for the night after having watched the animals in the pastures.

*pages 234–35
At the beginning of June, when the snow on the high passes has melted, the yak caravans loaded with grain return to Dolpo.*

Acknowledgments

The authors would like to thank the following: His Majesty King Birendra Bir Bikram Shah Dev; His Excellency G. P. Koirala, Prime Minister of Nepal; and Mr. Niranjan Koirala;

His Excellency R. H. Joshi, Minister of Tourism; the Ministry of the Interior; and the Department of Communications, for their help throughout the years;

The National Geographic Society, especially Gilbert M. Grosvenor, President and Chairman of the Board; William Graves, Editor; Bill Allen, Betsy Moize, Bob Poole, Allan Royce, Tom Kennedy, Tim Kelly, Kent Kobersteen, Jon Schneeburger, Connie H. Phelps, Peter Miller, Charlene Valeri, Pete Petrone, and many others for their confidence in us and for their encouragement.

The authors would also like to thank: NASA; the whole Leica team, and most particularly Doctors Bruno and Verena Frey, Von Zydowitz, Tina, Attila Von Gyimes, Nicole Rubbe and, of course, Yvon Plateau; Marie France and Jacques Yves de Rorthay, Michel Tallard, and the Vieux Campeur team; Summit Nepal, and especially Robin Marston, Gyani Bade, and Roger Henke; Colonel Penjor Ongdi and his whole family, as well as the staff of the Hati Ban Resort in Kathmandu; at RNAC, Moti KC and Tara Vezies, and all the team at Nepalganj and Juphal; Les and Una Douglas, Marinette Maviel, Jerome Edou, Martin Spice, Genevieve and Jo Couteau, Paul de Roujoux, Kalpana Ghimere; Nata Rampazzo and Benoit Nacci, as well as Hervé de La Martinière, our editor; special thanks to Lakpa Gyalzen Sherpa and Sylvain Bardoux, companions on all our Himalayan adventures; Tilen Lhundrup, Labrang Tundup, Lhundrup, Lama Norbu, Pema Kandro, Tsering Palmo, Karma, Renzing Dorje, Nanda Lal Thapa, Rupa Karki, and all our caravan friends. A sad goodbye to Puti Ongmo and Urgen, who recently died. Thanks above all to the gods of the Himalaya for their forbearance.

Technical Note: All photos were taken with Kodachrome 64 or with Kodachrome 200, sometimes pushed to ASA 500. The cameras used were Leicas—R5, R7, and M6. Leica lenses, from 19-mm to 280-mm, were sometimes used with a tele-converter.

About the Authors

Frenchman Eric Valli and Australian Diane Summers have lived in Nepal for a number of years and are fluent in the language of the country. They have traveled extensively in the Himalaya with their two young daughters, Sara and Camille, making a living by photographing and recording Asia's threatened traditional cultures. Their adventures range from documenting Gurung honey hunters dangling from 400-foot cliffs in the southwestern Himalayan foothills to trekking over some of the highest passes in the world with the yak caravanners of Dolpo. They have written and photographed articles for NATIONAL GEOGRAPHIC and published several books. Their familiarity with their chosen home, the deep friendships they have made in their travels, and the years they devote to each subject give their accounts a true insider's touch that harks back to the early days of exploration in these remote regions.

Back endpapers: The Himalaya seen from the space shuttle Columbia. *At right, the high Tibetan Plateau; at left, the plain of the Ganges.*

This book was printed at Kapp Lahure Jombart in Evreux, France, in September 1994.

Index

Illustrations are in **boldface**. Western names are inverted; Tibetan and Nepali names are not.

Amchis 19, 51-53, 56, **57**
Aphrodisiacs 101, 104
Arrow contests **24-25**, 26-27

Baga La, Nepal 126, 157, 158, **159**
Balkuna (deity) 197
Barley **122-123**; threshing **121**
Beans, red **187**, 196,
Bhotechaur, Nepal 206
Blacksmiths 61-65, **66-67**
Brahmaputra see Tsangpo
Buddhism, Tibetan 13, 30, 62, 153, 156; leaders **130**; see also Lamas; Monasteries
Budhi Dhami 176

Caravan trade 14-15, 46, 70-71; routes 6-7, 145, 205; see also Sheep caravans; Yak caravans
Castes 62, 64, 108, 188
Chagar La, Nepal 127, 142
Chakhure Lekh, Nepal, 204, 205, **212-213**, 220, **221**, 228
Chang 26, 27, 29, 61
Chang Tang, Tibet 12, 119, 120-121; pack animals 196-197
Changdzo chorten, Tinkyu, Nepal **40-41**
Chaudhabise, Nepal 180, 181, 196
Chenrezig mantra 142
Chetri (caste) 188, **218**
Chewong 139, 150
Chillums 176, **185**, 195-196, **205**
Chime Renzing 142, 184; wife 27
China: control of trans-Himalayan trade 120, 173, 176; invasion of Tibet 15, 119-120, 173
Cho-kyi **98**
Chogmis 108
Chopa Lhakhang, Phiger, Nepal 70
Chu gyen 43, **44-45**, 46
Chuma, Nepal 181, 229; grain husking **172**; shaman **191**
Cordyceps sinensis 99-101, 103-104, **104**

Creation myths: Tibet 69
Cremation 56

Da kurim (exorcism) 23, **24-25**, 26-27
Dailekh, Nepal **200-203**
Dalai Lama **130**
Daulakot, Nepal 219-221, 226-229
Dawa (daughter of Tilen) 139
Dawa (porter) **78**
DeCoursey, Maureen 103-104
Divination 22, 23, 52, 85, 88; book 88; Rong-pa 190-191, **191**, 192
Do, Nepal **112-113**
Doctors 19, 51-53, 56, **57**
Dokos **224-225**
Dolpo, Nepal: ban on foreign visitors 8, 11; first appearance on a map 14; first foreign visitor 11, 13, 14; food production 46; map **6-7**; traveler's offering 11-12
Dolpo-pa 206; greeting custom 118; housing 51, 56, 73, **112-113**, 132; last rites 74-75; trading partners 119-120, 173; see also Yak caravans; Yaks
Drabye, Lake, Tibet 118
Drakpo, Guru 30, **38-39**
Drok-pa 74; trade with Dolpo-pa 14-15, 118-121
Drolma (divinity) 153
Druptob Sangye Yeshe 71

Exorcism 23, **24-25**, 26-30, **38-39**, 88-90

Fadse 118
Fire tip treatment 52-53, **57**; Tibetan manual **50**

Gamoche monastery, Nepal 71
Garas 61-65, **66-67**
Gnichor Puti 108-109
Goats 196-197
Grain **122-123**, **172**, **177**; divination 190-191, **191**, 192; trade 14-15, 75, 79, 94, 119, 120, 173-186, 226-229, **230-231**, route 139
Guesar de Ling 26; song 31

Gurkha, kingdom of 14
Gyap shi 88-90

Hagen, Tony 13
Hermits 69-71
Himalayan Pilgrimage (Snellgrove) 14
Hinduism 14
Hurikot, Nepal 83, 173, 184

Indian Ocean: salt 173, 206, 226

Jakdula river, Nepal 79
Jamyang 99-101
Jest, Corneille 14
Jivan booti see Yarsa-kumbu
Jumla, kingdom of 14
Jumla, Nepal 79. 181
Juniper bushes 75, **146-147**

Kabre La, Nepal **86-87**
Kgar, Nepal **110-111**
Kagmara La, Nepal 79, 160
Kagyupa school 131, 133
Kailash, Mount, Tibet 84
Kal Das 190-191, **191**, 192
Karma (son of Tilen) 118, 153
Karma Chodzom 27, 52
Karma Chung Chung 79-84, **86-87**, 88-90
Karma Tenzing (caravanner) **138**
Karma Tenzing, Lama **134-135**
Karmapa **130**
Kathmandu Valley, Nepal 14
Kawaguchi, Ekai 11, 13, 14
Khung La, Tibet 119
Kimbu La, Nepal 152, **164-167**
Kudong rinsil 56
Kunsang 27
Kurim (exorcism) 23, **24-25**, 26-30, **38-39**
Kyato Chongra, Tibet 119

Labrang Tundup **20-21**, **44-45**, 53, **129**
Lagmo Shey Pass, Nepal 152, 156
Lakpa Gyalzen Sherpa 27, 79, 83, 85, 88-90, **129**

Lamas 29-30, **34-35**, **38-39**, **68**, 84, 85, 88-90, 95, 115, **134-135**; caravans 143-145, 153, 156; lamaseries **32-33**, 70
Leopards: threat to caravans 148, 156, 204, 205
Lho, kingdom of 14, 69
Lhu 88-90
Lhundrup 118, 139, 150, 153, 160

Makeup 29
Malla, kingdom of 205
Mantras: chenrezig 142
Map **6-7**
Margom monastery, Nepal 71
Matthiessen, Peter 15
Mendrup 28, 29, 30
Milarepa 131
Milarepa tanka **134-135**
Mo (divination) 22, 23, 52, 85, 88; book 88; Rong-pa 190-191, **191**, 192
Monasteries 27-30, **32-33**, **36-37**, **42**, 70-71, 131, 137
Muni Basnet 221, 226-227, **230-231**
Mustang, kingdom of 14, 69

Namdo, Nepal 51
Nanda Lal Thapa **184**, **185**, **193**, **194**, **208-209**
Naphakuna, Lama 84, 85, 88-90
Nepal: modern state 14; salt taxation 14
Norbu, Lama **134-135**
Nyelde plain, Nepal 126, 152, **157**
Nyima, Lama 95

Old Karma **24-25**, 26

Parme Tuwa 23, 115
Pema Kandro 93, 94
Pema Ongmo 115, 118
Pemal Angyal **164-165**
Pemar 93-94
Phiger, Nepal 70, 93, 108
Plowing **60**
Polyandry 102, 105, 108-109
Pritivin Narayan Shah 14
Puti Ongmo **92**, 94-95

Raja Marga 205
Rakpie 108-109
Reincarnation 62
Reling monastery, Nepal 71
Renzing Dorje 46, 83, **124**, 125-129, 144
Reuzen Tsultrin **68**
Rimi Valley, Nepal 173, 176-180
Rimpoche, Guru 13, 30
Ringmo, Lake, Nepal **168-169**
Ringmo, Nepal 126, 127
Ringmo Valley, Nepal 158
Rong-pa 75, 152, 173-181, **182-183**, 184-190; caravan routes 205; shepherd **189**; shoes **228**; temple 188, 190-192; villages 188; *see also* Sheep caravans
Rupa Kali **222-223**
Rupa Karki **208-211**

Saldang, Nepal 19, **48-49**, 126, **146-147**; ban on animals within village limits 46; grain **122-123**; water distribution 43, **44-45**, 46
Salt: Indian salt 173, 206, 226; sacks 114, **143**, 147-148, **153-155**, 156, 158-159; taxation 15; trade 75, 109, 118-121, 139, 173-186, **187**, 226, 229; weather forecasting 160
Schaller, George 15
Sheep 120-121, **194**; shearing **184**
Sheep caravans **182-183**, 195-197, **198-201**, 204-206, **207-217**, 219-221, **222-223**, 226-229, **232-233**
Shey Tulku 131-133, 136-137
Shimin, Nepal: barley threshing **121**
Shoes: Rong-pa **228**
Shuk-tsher Gompa, Nepal **42**
Shuk-tsher, Nepal **58-59**
Snellgrove, David 14
The Snow Leopard (Matthiessen) 15
Sonam Chopel 27
Sonam Lodro 70, 71
Summers, Diane **12**, **55**, 152
Survey of India 13

Talphi, Nepal **178-179**
Tapa Gaon, Nepal 173
Tarap Valley, Nepal **110-113**
Tawa, Nepal 115, 118
Tea: bricks 131

Tegyam monastery, Nepal 71
Three Years in Tibet (Kawaguchi) 13
Tibet: Chinese invasion 15, 119-120, 173; salt 118-120, 229
Tibetans: bathing habits 149; creation myth 69; greeting custom 80
Tik-pu **98**
Tilen Lhundrup **23**, **31**, **120**, **143**, **149**, **162-163**, **176**
Totcha **29**
Tsakang Gompa 131, 137
Tsangpo, Tibet-India-Bangladesh 12-13, 118-119
Tsering (son of Tundup) 52, 62-64
Tsering Palmo 99-102
Tsering Tashi 27, 29
Tsewang 84, 85, 90
Tsong-pa 74
Tsonga Renzing 70
Tsultria **12**
Tsurphu monastery, Tibet 133
Turap, a Valley in the Himalaya (Jest) 14

Valli, Camille 22
Valli, Eric **10**, **129**
Valli, Sara **18**, **23**, **31**; illness 19, 22-23, 26-30

Wangyal 160
Water distribution: ritual 43, **44-45**, 46
Wolves: threat to caravans 148, 205
Wool: Chang Tang sheep 120-121

Yak caravans 70, 73-75, 79-81, **91**, **110-111**, 118-121, 139-161, **162-171**, **234-235**
Yak-pas 80, 156
Yaks **72**, **76-77**, **124**; aphrodisiac 104; dri 94-95, **106-107**; dung 75, 145; effects of altitude 180-181; packsaddles 150-151; sacred yaks 74-75; suffocation of 62, **63**, drawing **64**
Yang-tsher Gompa, Nepal 26, 28, **32-33**, 70; worshiper **36-37**
Yarsa-kumbu 99-101, 103-104, **104**
Yerka 144